MEDIUM ÆVUM MONOGRAPHS
EDITORIAL COMMITTEE

K.P. CLARKE, A.J. LAPPIN,
N.F. PALMER, P. RUSSELL, C. SAUNDERS

MEDIUM ÆVUM MONOGRAPHS
XXXIII

FROM OLD ENGLISH TO OLD NORSE

A STUDY OF OLD ENGLISH TEXTS
TRANSLATED INTO OLD NORSE
WITH AN EDITION OF THE
ENGLISH AND NORSE VERSIONS
OF
ÆLFRIC'S *DE FALSIS DIIS*

by

John Frankis

The Society for the Study of Medieval Languages and
Literature

OXFORD · MMXVI

The Society for the Study of Medieval Languages
and Literature

http://mediumaevum.modhist.ox.ac.uk

© John Frankis, 2016

British Library Cataloguing in Publication Data
A catalogue record for this book is available from the
British Library

ISBN-13:

978-0-907570-41-7 (hb)
978-0-907570-27-1 (pb)
978-0-907570-56-1 (pdf e-bk)

CONTENTS

Preface vii
Abbreviations viii
Old English texts translated into Old Norse 1
Ælfric's *De falsis diis* and its ON translation: Introduction 3
The texts and the manuscripts ....
    (a)   Manuscripts of Ælfric's *De falsis diis* 7
    (b)   Ælfric's *De falsis diis* and associated works 10
    (c)   The ON translation in Hauksbók 16
The OE text from which the translation was made 23
The date and provenance of the ON translation of *De falsis diis* 31
The OE and ON texts of *De falsis diis* ....
    (a)   The portions of the OE text omitted from the translation 47
    (b)   The treatment of the portions translated 50
    (c)   Additions made in the ON text 56
    (d)   Some stylistic features of the translation........................... 61
Other texts in Hauksbók connected with Ælfric's works 65
The OE and ON texts of *De auguriis*
    (a)   Introductory... 69
    (b)   Comparative table of the OE and ON texts..................... 73
    (c)   Aspects of the ON *De auguriis*... 75
The OE and ON texts of the *Prose Phoenix* ....
    (a)   Introductory... 81
    (b)   Comparative table of the OE and ON texts..................... 90
The ON *De falsis diis* and later ON writing................................ 95
Conclusion 109
An edition of part of Ælfric's *De falsis diis* and ON translation 115
Select Glossary for the ON *De falsis diis*................................... 179
Bibliography 183

PREFACE

I have taken an intermittent interest in the Old Norse translation of Ælfric's *De falsis diis* since Pope drew attention to it in 1968. Long ago a grant from the University of Newcastle upon Tyne Research Fund facilitated the purchase of photocopies of relevant manuscripts. At a later date an initial draft of what I had written on the topic was read by Professor Hans Bekker-Nielsen of the University of Odense, who kindly suggested various improvements.

When I first began looking into the subject, Hauksbók and manuscripts of other relevant Old Norse works were still at the Danish Arnamagæan Institute and I was happily able to see them while enjoying the hospitality of my late parents-in-law in Copenhagen.

A paper on the influence of the Old Norse *De falsis diis* on early sagas of St Olaf was read at the Third International Saga Conference in Oslo in 1976 and material from this is included below.

I owe a particular debt to Dr Jonatan Pettersson of Stockholm University who read a more recent version of this study and made helpful suggestions for a range of improvements.

I am grateful to the editorial board of *Medium Ævum Monographs* for accepting this study for publication, and to the editor, Professor Anthony Lappin, for helping to get my typescript into an acceptable form. I owe a particular debt to Dr Stephen Pink for his assistance in the final stages of preparing a complicated typescript for publication.

My spelling of Old Norse names shows inconsistencies that some readers may find regrettable: when discussing the generalities of early medieval history and civilisation I use the commonly accepted English forms of names (Harald Bluetooth, Thor and so on); when dealing with specific Old Norse/Icelandic texts I may use the spelling of the original manuscripts or, where appropriate, normalised Old Icelandic orthography.

My debt to my wife Lone has increased steadily over many years and in recent years it has acquired a new dimension in my continual reliance on her expertise in the handling of computers.

ABBREVIATIONS

CH I	*Ælfric's Catholic Homilies: The First Series*, ed. Peter Clemoes, EETS ss 17 (Oxford, 1997)
CH II	*Ælfric's Catholic Homilies: The Second Series*, ed. Malcolm Godden, EETS ss 5 (London, 1979)
CH III	*Ælfric's Catholic Homilies: Introduction, Commentary and Glossary*, ed. Malcolm Godden, EETS ss 18 (Oxford, 2000)
EETS	Early English Text Society
H. edn	*Hauksbók: Udgiven efter de Arnamagnæanske Håndskrifter No. 371, 544, og 675, 4°, samt forskellige papirhåndskrifter af det Kongelige Nordiske Oldskriftselskab* [ed. Eiríkur Jónsson and Finnur Jónsson] (Copenhagen, 1892-6)
H. fac.	*Hauksbók: The Arnamagnaean Manuscripts 371 4°, 544 4° and 675 4°*, Manuscripta Islandica 5, ed. Jón Helgason (Copenhagen, 1960)
ÍF	Íslenzk Fornrit
Ker	N. R. Ker, *Catalogue of Manuscripts containing Anglo-Saxon* (Oxford, 1957)
Legendary Saga	*Óláfs saga hins helga*, ed. O. A. Johnsen (Christiania, 1922)
LS I-II	*Ælfric's Lives of Saints*, ed. Walter W. Skeat, EETS os 76, 82, 94 and 114 (London, 1881-1900, repr. as 2 vols, London, 1966)
MGH	Monumenta Germaniae Historica
Script. rer. Ger.	Scriptores rerum Germanicarum
Script. rer. Merov.	Scriptores rerum Merovingicarum
OE	Old English
ON	Old Norse
PL	*Patrologia Latina*, ed. J.-P. Migne, 221 vols (Paris, 1844-65)
Pope	*Homilies of Ælfric: A Supplementary Collection*, ed. John C. Pope, EETS os 259 and 260, 2 vols (London, 1967-68)

OLD ENGLISH TEXTS TRANSLATED INTO OLD NORSE

A number of medieval manuscripts include texts in Old Norse-Icelandic that seem to be based on, and may in varying degrees be translated from, originals written in Old English. The present study aims to consider these to see what can be deduced about their origins and history. One text stands out as being clearly a substantial work of translation, the Old Norse version of Ælfric's Old English homily, *De falsis diis*, and this constitutes the starting point and centrepiece of the study, but other texts, though brief or fragmentary, are included in the study because of the light they throw on the circumstances of translation. The study includes an edition of the part of Ælfric's Old English homily for which a translation is extant, arranged in parallel with the Old Norse translation in order to facilitate comparison. Each text is accompanied by textual notes and a modern English translation of the text as edited and there is a select Old Norse glossary.

ÆLFRIC'S *DE FALSIS DIIS* AND ITS OLD NORSE TRANSLATION: INTRODUCTION

From the earlier Middle Ages before the twelfth century there are numerous texts translated from Latin into the vernaculars of northern Europe, particularly into Old English (OE) and Old High German, the principle vernacular languages to achieve literary status and the only ones to develop a tradition of sustained prose-writing before the twelfth century. Familiar examples include the translations of Boethius, *De consolatione philosophiae*, by king Alfred into OE and by Notker into Old High German; an important part of OE prose writing, and much verse too, consists of translations or adaptations from Latin. In all these cases the direction of translation was from Latin into the translator's own language, and, at the risk of stating the obvious, one could say that translation into the translator's mother-tongue was the commonest form for literary translation to take. Nevertheless, there are examples of translation in the opposite direction, one of the most notable being the tenth-century translation of the *Anglo-Saxon Chronicle* into Latin by *ealdormann* Æðelweard, all the more remarkable for being the work of a layman.

The twelfth century saw the rise of French as a literary language, and the international preeminence that it rapidly developed appears in the number of translations from French into English, German, Old Norse (ON) and other languages from the thirteenth century onwards. From before 1200, however, translations from one vernacular into another are very rare in surviving records. Much attention has been justifiably paid to the OE poem *Genesis B*, translated from Old Saxon, probably in the ninth century; complete texts of the original and of the translation have however not survived and the overlap between the extant Old Saxon and OE versions is only twenty-six lines. Less attention has been paid to one other early example, almost certainly pre-1200, of intra-vernacular translation, the ON version of Ælfric's OE homily, *De falsis diis*, though its existence has been recognised since the late nineteenth century. The reason for this neglect was that Ælfric's homily survives in several manuscripts, in most of which it is incomplete, and for a long time only fragments of the whole had appeared in print; and though these were sufficient to show that there was some connection with an ON text in Hauksbók, the precise nature of the connection was unclear. The best known printed excerpts were all from a portion of Ælfric's homily that was based on the *De correctione rusticorum* by Martin of Braga, so it seemed reasonable to assume that the ON text was translated from the same Latin source, though perhaps with cross-reference to the OE text. This possible, if only partial, use of an English text by a Norse writer was noted by Caspari in his edition of Martin of Braga and by several subsequent scholars, but it was not thoroughly investigated.[1]

Work on establishing the canon of Ælfric's writings and classifying the manuscripts progressed steadily and the results were summarised in an important study by Peter Clemoes and in Ker's magisterial *Catalogue*.[2] Even so, studies published in the early nineteen-sixties still maintained that the ON text was not primarily indebted to Ælfric.[3] The matter was settled in 1968 when J. C. Pope's edition of Ælfric's unpublished homilies finally made available the full text of *De falsis diis* and discussed the ON text in Hauksbók, showing conclusively that it was translated from the OE text

---

[1] *Martin von Bracaras Schrift*, ed. Caspari, p. cxxii; Bugge, *Studien*, I.11, n. 1; Turville-Petre, *Myth*, p. 95 and n. 7. Published extracts of Ælfric's homily were based mostly on MSS W and S and were restricted to the opening section: MS W was used by Unger, *Annaler* and *The Anglo-Saxon Dialogues of Salomon and Saturn*, ed. Kemble, II. 120; MS S by Kluge, *Angelsächsisches Lesebuch*, XIV(3); MS Xk by Müllenhof, 'Zur Deutschen Mythologie', p. 407, and printed in facsimile by Dubois, *Ælfric*, pp. 84 (Pl. II) and 363. The extract in MS G was used by Förster, *Altenglisches Lesebuch*, p. 31, and printed complete in *Early English Homilies*, ed. Warner, pp. 38-41, but was not recognised as part of *De falsis fiis* until identified by Ker, p. lxiv.

[2] Clemoes, 'The Chronology'; *Ker*, which actually has no entry for *De falsis diis* in the Index and summarises the manuscripts only under 'Kluge 1897' (Index, p. 533).

[3] See the otherwise valuable study by J. Turville-Petre, 'Sources', p. 175 n. 1, and Holtsmark, *Studier i Snorres Mytologi*, p. 11.

and not from any Latin original, for the compelling reason that there is in fact no single Latin source, while the translation includes passages that are original to Ælfric.[4] Ælfric freely combines a number of sources, including Martin of Braga and the Bible, as well as several other works, and the ON text follows the OE reasonably closely, with considerable omissions, minor additions and slight changes, but with clear verbal reminiscences in many places. As Pope points out, there is no evidence for the existence of any Latin work combining these diverse materials in this order that could have served as a common source for independent OE and ON translations. Attention had previously been focused on the passages of OE and ON that derive from Martin of Braga's *De correctione rusticorum*, but Ælfric's text comprises much more than that, and the correspondences between the English and Norse texts extend far beyond the portion dependent on Martin of Braga. Moreover, as is shown below, the matter is put beyond doubt by numerous verbal echoes from the OE original in the ON translation, and also by some striking misinterpretations of the OE text, where the translator could have solved his difficulties by consulting Latin sources if he had known of them.

After the appearance of Pope's edition a comparison of the OE and ON texts became easier: a preliminary study was published by Arnold Taylor and further studies have since appeared.[5] There is no firm evidence about the date and place of the translation but it has generally been assumed without question that the work is Icelandic; this assumes that a manuscript of the homily was taken to Iceland where it was seen by someone who was able to translate it and valued it highly enough to undertake this task, a somewhat problematic series of suppositions. As I attempt to show, circumstantial evidence, particularly concerning manuscript production

---

[4] *Pope* no. XXI, ll. 667-724, esp. pp. 669-70; Pope points to phrases in the Norse text that exactly translate phrases in Ælfric for which there is no Latin source: see his note on line 483.

[5] Taylor, '*Hauksbók*'. Abram, 'Anglo-Saxon homilies', pp. 436-37.

and circulation, gives little support to this assumption and points to another possibility that is explored here.

It is hoped that the parallel-text edition offered here will clarify further details and make it easier to evaluate the whole textual situation, as well as providing firmer ground for considering the question of the historical and social milieux that produced, preserved and transformed the translation.

The circumstances of the translation are further clarified by taking into account two other OE texts for which there is evidence of translation into ON; it is unlikely that all these texts, which share circumstances of manuscript circulation, should have been translated independently, and this activity is most plausibly ascribed to an English milieu in which work was in progress on the preservation, renovation and adaptation of OE texts. One might further be inclined to assume that the target language, ON, was, according to the commonest pattern, the translator's mother-tongue; this may well have been the case, but examples of translation from the mother-tongue into another language make such an assumption unsafe, and the language of the texts concerned gives no clear clues as to the translator's background. The linguistic situation in eleventh and twelfth-century England may have some bearing on this matter.

In the ON *De falsis diis* different kinds of translation can be detected and the other texts considered are problematic in various ways, but all include at least short passages of close translation. Considered in the wider context of translations in general one can say that while the source texts are fairly clear, though not unarguable, there is some uncertainty as to whether there is anything that can firmly be called a target text, though the translator presumably had a target. The translation process here is nebulous and the end result, less a target than an accidental outcome, raises various questions; what kind of bearing these texts might have on Translation Theory must be for someone else to determine.

THE TEXTS AND THE MANUSCRIPTS

(a) Manuscripts of Ælfric's *De falsis diis*

The relevant factors are summarised here from Ker's *Catalogue* (*Ker*) and from Pope's edition (*Pope*, pp. 1-93 and 673-75), where fuller information may be found: anyone wishing to undertake further work on the genesis and interpretation of this homily will need to refer to these two publications.

Ælfric's *De falsis diis* is preserved in varying forms in seven manuscripts, but most of these contain only an incomplete text.[6] When referring to the OE homily in the present discussion, line-numbers will, where appropriate, be those in Pope's edition of Ælfric's complete text and these are prefixed with P (in Pope's edition the homily consists of 676 lines); line-numbers without this P-prefix refer to the parallel-text edition given below, which omits the final part of the OE text for which no ON translation is extant; this edition has its own line-numbering in order to facilitate detailed comparison of the two texts. References to the ON text in this edition are prefixed with H.

Ælfric's homily *De falsis diis* is preserved in part or in whole in the following manuscripts, here listed in approximate chronological order; information on these manuscripts, including dates of compilation, is from *Ker* (to which reference is given), supplemented from Clemoes *CH* I, 1-64.

W   London, British Library, MS Cotton Julius E.VII (s.xi in: *Ker* 162; unknown origin, in Bury St Edmunds in s.xiii), fols 238-40v: lines P1-191, excepting P141-49 (the end of the manuscript, presumably containing the rest of the text, is now missing).

R   Cambridge, Corpus Christi College, MS 178 (s.xi^1: *Ker* 41; ?Worcester), pp. 142-63: complete excepting lines P314-17.

Xk   Paris, Bibliothèque Nationale, MS Lat. 7585 (s.xi^1: *Ker* 366), fol. 238v: lines P104-52, excepting P141-49.

---

[6] The sigla for manuscripts of Ælfric's works were devised by Clemoes, 'Chronology'; they are listed in in *Pope*, p. xvii, and the classification summarised on pp. 6-14.

C   Cambridge, Corpus Christi College, MS 303 (s.xii¹: *Ker* 57; ?Rochester), pp. 306-17: complete excepting lines P141-49 and P515-64.

S   Oxford, Bodleian Library, MS Hatton 116 (s.xii¹: *Ker* 333; W. Midland), pp. 365-73: lines P1-150 and P644-76.

G   London, British Library, MS Cotton Vespasian D.XIV (s.xii med: *Ker* 209; ?Canterbury or Rochester), fols 40-48v: lines P302-498.

L   Cambridge, University Library, MS Ii. 1. 33 (s.xii²: *Ker* 18; ?Canterbury), fols 175v-84v: lines P1-543, excepting lines P141-49.

The extract in Xk is short and also much abridged and partly paraphrased: it is a fairly drastic rewriting of a short portion of Ælfric's text; it is of interest as an early adaptation of Ælfric but it has no textual value: it was adapted as a brief OE note on pagan gods added at the end of an earlier Latin manuscript of Isidore's *Etymologiae*. The extract in G is added to part of another homily by Ælfric (*CH* II, homily no. xxxiii) to form a new work and hence is of restricted textual importance. The other five manuscripts are all important, even though two of them, S and W, contain only a small part of the homily. Pope points out that these five manuscripts fall into two groups, CLW and RS, the last two being characterised by the inclusion of a passage (lines P141-49) that is not in the others; he plausibly argues that CLW represent the original version of the homily, while RS contain an addition made by Ælfric himself; the authenticity of the added lines, P141-49, is attested by the fact that Wulfstan drew on them when writing his own abridged version of Ælfric's homily.[7]

The most obvious thing about these manuscripts is that they are all, with one exception, manuscripts containing various collections of Ælfric's homilies; the exception, Xk,

---

[7]   See *The Homilies of Wulfstan*, ed. Bethurum, no. XII, pp. 221-24; this is a rewriting of Ælfric's *De falsis diis*, lines 72-165, and was cited by some earlier scholars as a source of the ON text in Hauksbók. The ON text is in fact clearly based on Ælfric's homily and contains material not in Wulfstan's abridgement.

has merely a brief quotation, adapted perhaps as a mnemonic note. MS G, an interestingly eccentric collection, includes some later works not by Ælfric, but most of its contents are homilies by Ælfric. There is in fact no reason to believe that the OE *De falsis diis* ever circulated in isolation, and, as will eventually appear below, the ON translation seems originally to have been part of a small collection of adaptations into ON of works by, or associated by scribes with, Ælfric.

It is noteworthy that four of these seven manuscripts are actually post-conquest copies of the texts concerned, showing that an interest in Anglo-Saxon religious writing was maintained for over a century after the Norman conquest.

Nevertheless, apart from the varying degrees of completeness of the homily in surviving manuscripts, and the added lines in RS, there is relatively little textual variation among the five main manuscripts, and even G is a relatively faithful copy of the portion used (Xk however is not). Indeed, the high level of agreement between these manuscripts is a remarkable testimony to the accuracy of copyists over a period of nearly two hundred years. In consequence, any attempt at selecting a version that comes closest to that used by the translator into ON is bound to depend on minor details of a fairly inconclusive kind. Pope was clearly right to take R as the basis of his edition: it is the earliest complete manuscript and contains a text that must be closer than any other to Ælfric's final intention for this homily. The edition offered here, however, is based on C because in certain details explained below this manuscript corresponds most closely to that used by the translator. It is to be hoped that an edition of a hitherto unprinted twelfth-century version of Ælfric's homily, such as may have been used by the translator, may be of more interest than a simple reprint of Pope's excellent and well-known text, even though the final part of the homily (incomplete in C) is omitted here because there is no extant translation of it.

(b) Ælfric's *De falsis diis* and associated works

This work does not belong to any of Ælfric's major sequences of homilies, the *Catholic Homilies* and the *Lives of Saints*.[8] MS W is incidentally the best manuscript of Ælfric's *Lives of Saints* and the basis of Skeat's edition, and its compiler included *De falsis diis* in that manuscript; *De falsis diis* is in no sense a saint's life but it has important themes in common with many of Ælfric's saints' lives that deal with the triumph of early Christians over paganism; Skeat did not however include it in his edition of *LS*. *De falsis diis* appears in MS W beside certain other texts that are likewise not saints' lives; one of these, the homily *In laetania maiore* (commonly referred to as *De auguriis*), was printed by Skeat as no. xvii (*LS* I.364-83): traces of an ON translation of this also appear in Hauksbók and are discussed below. Other works appended to the saints' lives in W are Ælfric's translations of Alcuin's *Interrogationes Sigewulfi* and (according to the original table of contents, though no longer extant in this manuscript, from which the final portion has been lost) of *De duodecim abusivis*.[9] These four texts form a group that recurs, not necessarily consecutively, in other manuscripts, as shown in the following table (the numbers below the manuscript sigla refer to the article within Ker's description of the manuscript).

---

[8] *CH I, II, III, LS I, II*; *CH III* contains an authoritative sketch of Ælfric's career with references to relevant recent studies.

[9] 'Ælfric's version of *Alcuini interrogationes Sigeuulfi in Genesin*', ed. MacLean. At the time of writing there was no complete edition of *De duodecim abusivis*, and *Two Ælfric Texts: 'The Twelve Abuses' and 'The Vices and Virtues'*, ed. and trans. Clayton, appeared too late for me to make use of it. The text from MS R was printed in *Old English Homilies*, ed. Morris, pp. 296-304 (with an early ME transcription from MS Lambeth 487 on pp. 101-19); the text from MS G is in *Early English Homilies*, pp. 11-19. On these texts see Clemoes, 'Chronology', pp. 220 and 239, n. 3. Aspects of the textual history of *De auguriis* are discussed by Hill, 'The dissemination of Ælfric's *Lives of Saints*', p. 252 and n. 61.

Text and Manuscripts

MSS:	G	L	C	W	R	S	P
Interrogationes Sigewulfi	—	—	66	48	3	18	32
De duodecim abusivis	6	—	63	*50	7	19	
De auguriis	—	38	47	22	8	20	
De falsis diis	15	34	65	49	18	21	—

(Note: W*50 is a token number for the piece recorded in the original table of contents but subsequently lost from the manuscript.)

MS P, Oxford, Bodleian Library, MS Hattton 115 (s.xii²: *Ker* 332), is included here because it has so much in common with R and S (see *Pope* pp. 53-59), although it does not contain *De falsis diis*. *De auguriis* occurs altogether in eight manuscripts (listed in *Ker*, p. 529), five of which (LCWRS) also contain *De falsis diis*. The four texts named here are the only pieces that appear in all four manuscripts CWRS, and as Pope points out (p. 65) R and S stand apart from the others because they contain added matter, not only in *De falsis diis* (P141-49) but also in *De auguriis* (the addition is printed as *Pope* no. XXIX) and in *Interrogationes Sigewulfi* (see *Pope* pp. 454-59). These four texts that so regularly occur together may have been seen by copyists as serving a basic evangelical purpose for clerics, whether secular or monastic, in a society where Christianity was perceived as not yet universally established, though Ælfric need not have had this purpose in mind in writing them and may not have intended them to constitute a group. *De falsis diis* is a condemnation of idolatry, *De auguriis* is a condemnation of superstition, *De duodecim abusivis* asserts a basic Christian morality, and *Interrogationes Sigewulfi* expounds the foundations of Christian doctrine from the opening chapters of Genesis, concluding with a discourse on the Trinity (though this section may not have been intended for this context by Ælfric).

Ælfric's authorship of *De falsis diis* is uncontested and it was probably written in the years around, or just before,

1000.¹⁰ It takes the form of an attack on idolatry and may have been prompted by the belief, reflected in other texts from the period 990-1015 such as *The Battle of Maldon* and Wulfstan's *Sermo Lupi ad Anglos*, that paganism was widespread among the Scandinavian invaders of England who accompanied king Svein Forkbeard of Denmark in the late tenth century.¹¹ This belief may reflect an uncritical habit of mind surviving from the Scandinavian attacks of a century earlier but there may also have been some truth in it. Svein's father, king Harald Bluetooth, famously claimed on the Jelling stone (probably about 960-80) that he had made the Danes Christian; the veracity of this claim is impossible to verify of course, but it may be assumed that Svein and most of his Danish followers regarded themselves as Christians, and Svein's son Cnut became, as king of England, a generous, even ostentatious, patron of the church. Many Norwegians however were still pagans in the late tenth century, and there were certainly Norwegians who took part in the Danish invasion. According to the Anglo-Saxon Chronicle, Anlaf, usually taken to be Olaf Tryggvason of Norway, accompanied Svein in his attack on England in 991, but he withdrew after being baptised under Æthelred's sponsorship in 994 and his later attempts to enforce Christianity in Norway met with a good deal of opposition from those of his subjects who were still pagan. Twenty years later Olaf Haraldsson likewise had problems with enforcing Christianity in Norway after his baptism in 1014, so one can be reasonably sure that Christianity had not become as widespread in Norway as it had in Denmark by the begin-

---

[10] See Clemoes, 'Chronology'; *Pope*, p. 147, suggests a slightly earlier date at the end of the tenth century.

[11] In *The Battle of Maldon* (presumably written in the last decade of the tenth century or soon after) the invaders are described as *hæðene*, 'heathens' (55 and 181): see *The Battle of Maldon*, ed. Scragg, with a discussion of the historical background on pp. 9-14; Wulfstan's *Sermo Lupi* (written in 1014) has several references to heathen people and heathen customs in England, presumably referring to newly arrived Scandinavian invaders: see *Sermo Lupi ad Anglos*, ed. Whitelock, lines 26-36 and 140 and n., and introduction pp. 11-12.

ning of the eleventh century, and this (together with the probably pagan Swedish component in the armies of Svein and Cnut) may have encouraged a widespread view in early eleventh-century England that all the Scandinavian invaders were pagans.[12] No doubt it was also politically convenient for some English leaders to encourage the view that the Scandinavian invaders were pagans so that resistance became a matter of religious as well as of national principle. Ælfric's homily against idolatry may therefore have had some contemporary relevance in strengthening the faith of his audience in the years around 1000. Beside this view of the homily's historical context it may be argued however that attacks on paganism are recurrent in patristic writings and sometimes give the impression that the writer is repeating established themes even though they may not have had much contemporary relevance to the people addressed by the writer. Attacks on paganism figure prominently in early saints' lives, including many of those by Ælfric, and *De falsis diis*, like many saints' lives, is probably as much a celebration of a past triumph as a warning against a present peril. As Pope points out, its terms are general and seem to have little reference to contemporary life in England, in marked contrast, for example, to Wulfstan's *Sermo Lupi ad Anglos*. Even Ælfric's use of the ON names of the pagan deities Thor, Odin and Frigg, which at first glance looks like a reference to contemporary practice and belief among the Scandinavian invaders of England, should not quite be taken at face-value: it reveals no knowledge of actual Scandinavian paganism, only the names of three gods. In this passage Ælfric is paraphrasing Martin of Braga's *De correctione rusticorum* and the names of Scandinavian deities are introduced to explain Martin's attack on classical paganism. Furthermore, even Martin's attack cannot be taken as giving reliable information about the actuality of sixth-century paganism in the areas where Martin was active (southern Gaul and the

---

[12] Townend, *Language and History*, pp. 134-38, presents evidence to substantiate this. On paganism in Norway see Abram, *Myths of the Pagan North*, pp. 123-81.

Iberian peninsula, where the orthodox Christianity of the native population was as much in conflict with the Arianism of the Visigothic invaders as with any vestigial paganism). As Martin makes clear, the pagan deities named represent the seven planets of the Ptolemaic cosmography (Sun, Moon, Mars, Mercury, Jupiter, Venus and Saturn), after whom the days of the week came to be named in Latin. The English names of the days of the week, however they had originally been arrived at, provided writers like Ælfric with a simple and familiar formula for naming the northern counterparts of the corresponding classical deities, though, as Pope points out (pp. 668-69), it is striking that Ælfric gave the ON names of the gods (*Oðon, Þor, Fricg,* representing Óðinn, Þórr and Frigg) rather than the OE names (Woden, Þunor, Frige) that were perpetuated in the English names of the days of the week. Why Ælfric omitted naming an equivalent for Mars (ON Týr) is unclear: perhaps, for whatever reason, he had not come across the ON name. Presumably it suited Ælfric's purpose to encourage the idea that these were specifically Scandinavian pagan gods, implying that many Scandinavians were still pagans, and he had no wish to remind his audience that English speech preserved in the names of the days of the week (including *Tiwesdæg* for *Martis dies*) an apparently respectful record of an extinct native paganism. In so far as the homily contains an attack on specifically Norse paganism, and it is only a minor element in the whole work, it may have been encouraged by a more general distrust of foreign ways and manners, like the attack on Danish fashions in clothing in the 'Letter to Brother Edward', a text contemporary with (and in Pope's opinion, possibly by) Ælfric.[13]

De falsis diis opens with a short prose introduction on the doctrine of the Trinity (P1-24) and then continues in Ælfric's

---

[13] Oxford, Bodleian Library, MS Hatton 115, fols 60-61, printed by Kluge, 'Fragment eines angelsächsischen Briefes'; partly translated in *English Historical Documents*, ed. Whitelock, no. 232, p. 896. This text is preserved in MSS R and P and is thus in some degree peripheral to *De falsis diis* and the other texts listed above: see *Pope*, pp. 56-57.

characteristic rhythmic prose, based on a four-stressed line-structure similar to that of OE verse.[14] The homily is then in four sections:–

> Section I (P25-209): the general features of paganism regarded as a fall from paradisal perfection: Paradise and the Fall (P25-71), the rise of idolatry as related in Genesis (P72-98), classical paganism interpreted in Norse terms (P99-180), and a denunciation of idolatry (P181-209). This section is based on part of Martin of Braga's *De correctione rusticorum*.[15]
>
> Section II (P210-493): Old Testament stories of God's victories over paganism and idolatry: Dagon and the Ark of the Covenant, from 1 Samuel (Vulgate, I Regum), chs 4-7 (P210-91); Daniel's first imprisonment in the lions' den, from the Book of Daniel, chs 5-6 (P292-349); Daniel and Bel, from the apocryphal Book of Daniel and Bel (Vulgate, Book of Daniel, ch. 14), verses 1-21 (P350-431); Daniel and the dragon, with the second imprisonment in the lions' den and the miracle of Habakkuk, from the same source, verses 22-42 (P432-493).
>
> Section III (P494-520): a linking passage on the Sixth Age of the World and the change brought about by the incarnation of Christ.
>
> Section IV (P521-676): examples of Christian victories over paganism and idolatry: the overthrow of the idol of Serapis in Alexandria, chiefly from Cassiodorus, *Historia tripartita* IX. 27-8 (P521-71); the defeat of Apollo by Gregory the Thaumaturgist, from Rufinus's addition to his translation of Eusebius, *Ecclesiastical History* VII. 28 (P572-648); and a conclusion asserting the divinity of Christ against the objection that pagan gods had seniority (P649-76).

The extant ON translation corresponds to Sections I and II but only part of III, omitting IV entirely; reasons for assuming that the whole of Ælfric's homily may originally have

---

[14] On Ælfric's rhythmical prose see *Pope*, pp. 105-35; Blake, 'Rhythmic alliteration', objects to a term that classsifies as prose a literary form that is neither verse nor prose.

[15] See *Martin von Bracaras Schrift*; *Martini episcopi Bracarensis opera omnia*, ed. Barlow, pp. 159-203. For a translation of Martin's homily see Herlihy, ed., *Medieval Culture and Society*, pp. 33-42. Ælfric's use of Martin is discussed by Pope, who prints relevant extracts as footnotes.

been translated and later subjected to abridgement are discussed below.

(c) The Old Norse translation in Hauksbók

Surviving copies of Ælfric's *De falsis diis* were written down at various times during a period of nearly two hundred years (early eleventh to late twelfth centuries), but even more time elapsed before the only extant copy of the ON translation was committed to writing in the early fourteenth century. Hauksbók (here referred to as H), one of the dozen most important ON manuscripts extant today, is named after the only identifiable writer to contribute to it, Haukr Erlendsson (c.1260-1334). Haukr was an Icelander by birth and had risen to become Lawman of Iceland by 1294; shortly after this he moved to Norway under the patronage of king Hákon Magnússon, where he became Lawman of Oslo in 1302 and later of the Gulaþing in Bergen. Norway was thus Haukr's place of residence after about 1300, and, though he visited Iceland in 1306-8 and perhaps again in 1330-1, he died in Norway in 1334.

The manuscript that bears his name consists of three separate parts, AM 371 4° (18 leaves), AM 544 4° (107 leaves), and AM 675 4° (16 leaves), now held in the Árni Magnússon Institute in Reykjavik (Stofnun Árna Magnússonar á Íslandi). It is written partly in Haukr's own hand and partly by a number of unidentified contributors (fifteen different hands have been distinguished). Haukr himself wrote the opening section (AM 371 4°, fols 1-18) and also made occasional additions at various points in the main portion (AM 544 4°).[16] This portion was evidently available for contributions by various hands, including that of Haukr; this was formerly taken to imply that it was maintained in Haukr's household in Norway by a circle of his associates,

---

[16] Fundamental for any study is *H. edn*, a detailed and accurate transcription of the whole manuscript. For the structure of Hauksbók and the hands involved see the introduction to *H. fac*. More recent studies are summarised in Pulsiano and Wolf, eds, *Medieval Scandinavia*, p. 271.

who included both Norwegians and Icelanders, and this is borne out by the mixed forms of language throughout, as well as the mixture of materials of Icelandic and Norwegian origin. Haukr was resident in Norway during most of the time when the manuscript was being compiled, so its compilation was commonly thought to have taken place in Norway. It has been suggested however that the manuscript was compiled in Iceland about the time of Haukr's visit in 1306-08, and present-day scholarly opinion probably inclines rather to this view, though the evidence is inconclusive.[17] It is presumably possible to reconcile these apparently conflicting views if one postulates that AM 544, with its mixed Icelandic and Norwegian materials and forms of language, was compiled in Haukr's household in Norway and was then taken by him to Iceland in 1306, where he wrote AM 371, with its purely Icelandic texts, and that he left both manuscripts there when he returned to Norway in 1308 (how AM 675 should be incorporated into this hypothesis would remain to be determined). But this hypothesis may seem implausibly elaborate and there is no firm evidence.

Taylor assumed that the translation of *De falsis diis* was made in Iceland but there is no evidence for that other than the preservation there of Hauksbók; for reasons explained below, I think the translation was probably made in England for transmission to Norway, but it eventually had some circulation in Iceland, and the exact circumstances of its copying into Hauksbók are not crucial to my argument here. In any case, the manuscript was compiled during the first two decades of the fourteenth century and the main period of Anglo-Norwegian contacts was over by then.

There had been numerous contacts between England and Denmark and Norway in the pre-conquest period and these continued after the conquest, particularly with Norway;

---

[17] Studies of the language are listed and summarised in *H. fac.*, pp. x-xii. Karlsson, 'Aldur Hauksbókar', suggests that the manuscript may have been compiled in Iceland as it is first recorded there about 1600 and, since portions of the book can be dated to 1302-10, Haukr's contributions could have been made during his visit to Iceland in 1306-08.

there seems however to be rather less evidence of direct contacts between England and Iceland.[18] Contacts between England and Norway, particularly ecclesiastical, continued to be plentiful throughout the great period of Norwegian vernacular writing under the patronage of Hákon Hákonarson (1216-1263), but under Eiríkr Magnússon (1280-1299) English connections were largely replaced by German as the Hanseatic treaty of 1287, which gave exclusive trading rights to German merchants, made Norway much less accessible to English shipping. This seems to have affected the whole range of contacts, including ecclesiastical, which had largely ceased by the end of the thirteenth century. The surviving copy of the ON translation of *De falsis diis* was therefore written down in a society that no longer had close contacts with England and it is unlikely that the scribe who copied it into Hauksbók had any knowledge of its history and provenance. Before this the translated text must have undergone copying and revision, perhaps repeatedly, so that any peculiarities of language that the original may have had were eliminated in this process: conjectures concerning the date and place of translation are therefore much less firmly based than might have been the case if there had been an extant copy closer in time to the translator.

The contents of Hauksbók are varied, including prose and verse, religious and secular texts, and works of Norwegian and Icelandic origin. It is famous for its texts of important Icelandic works: *Landnámabók* and several sagas, including *Hervarar saga*, *Fóstbrœðra saga* and *Eiríks saga rauða*; its text of *Völuspá* is of great importance, whatever its ultimate place of origin. It also contains numerous works of medieval learning in ON translation, some certainly Icelandic, some of Norwegian origin: not only narratives like *Trójumanna saga* and *Breta saga* (the ON translations of Dares Phrygius and

---

[18] The classic studies of Anglo-Scandinavian contacts, Taranger, *Den angelsaksiske Kirkes*, and Leach, *Angevin Britain and Scandinavia*, still contain much of value. See further Kolsrud, *Noregs Kyrkjesoga*, pp. 124-26 and 150-51. More recent studies are listed and summarised in Abrams, 'The Anglo-Saxons'; see also Abrams, 'Eleventh-century missions'.

Geoffrey of Monmouth respectively), but also such standard educational texts as *Algorismus* and the *Elucidarius* ascribed to Honorius of Autun, which is generally believed to have been composed in post-conquest England.

The first two items in the book, occupying the present MS AM 371 4°, are specifically Icelandic texts, *Landnámabók* and *Kristni saga*, copied by Haukr himself; the second part, the present MS AM 544 4°, opens in a new hand with a collection of assorted pieces of medieval learning to which *H. edn* gives the titles *Heimslýsing ok helgifræði* and *Heimspeki ok helgifræði*.[19] It is perhaps misleading to give either of these sections a title that could be taken to imply a unified work: each is a collection of more or less disconnected pieces, having something of the character of a medieval commonplace-book, in which the principal unifying factor is that the separate pieces were of interest to the compiler who recorded them, though he may well have been motivated by the considerations described by Sverrir Jakobsson. The first of these collections, *Heimslýsing*, is copied by someone identified in *H. fac.* as 'the first Norwegian hand' and it is the main concern of the present study; it consists of separate chapters with manuscript headings, to which *H. edn* has added chapter-numbers from 1 to 18. In the case of chapters 5 and 6 the two chapter-numbers have been given erroneously (in spite of the lack of the customary large initial capital for the alleged chapter 6) to what is in fact one continuous item, the translation of Ælfric's *De falsis diis*.

The contents of *Heimslýsing* in AM 544 4° are as follows:

fol. 1r, ch. 1 (no title): a list of rivers of the world.

fol. 1v, ch. 2 *Prologus*: a list of historians, biblical and classical.

fol. 2r, ch. 3 *Fra paradiso*: the rivers of paradise.

---

[19] A valuable study of this part of the manuscript is Jakobsson, 'Hauksbók', though he overlooks (p. 31) some differences between *De falsis diis* and the introduction to *Trójumanna saga*: the former does not identify Saturn with Freyr or Venus with Freyja; see however n. 108 below.

fol. 2r, ch. 4   *Her segir fra þvi hversu lond liggia i veroldinni*: the marvels of the east.

fol. 4r, chs 5-6   *Um þat hvaðan otru hofst*, 'On the origins of false belief', translated from Ælfric's *De falsis diis*, P1-499.

fol. 8r, ch. 7   *Fra þvi hvar hverr Noa sona bygði heimin*, 'On how each of Noah's sons settled the earth'.

fol. 8v, ch. 8   *Her segir fra marghattaðum þioðum*: an account of various races and monsters.

fol. 9v, ch. 9   *Her segir* .... (illegible): a homily on superstitions, ascribed to Augustine, partly based on Ælfric's *De auguriis*.

fol. 10v, ch. 10   *Her segir hvaðan blot skurguða hofust*: on the origin of idolatry, translated from *Elucidarius* II.21.

fol. 11r, ch. 11   *Her segir fra draumum*: on dreams, from *Elucidarius* III.9.

fol. 11r, ch. 12   *Her segir fra Antichristo*: from *Elucidarius* III.10.

fol. 11v, ch. 13   *Um uprisu kvicra oc dauða*: from *Elucidarius* III.11, paragraphs 1, 2, 4 and 5 only.

fol. 12r, ch. 14   *Um imbrudaga hald*: homily on Ember Days.

fol. 13r, ch. 15   *Um regnboga*: allegorical interpretation of the colours of the rainbow.

fol. 13v, ch. 16   *Um solstoðr*: on the solstices.

fol. 13v, ch. 17   *Um uppstigning solar oc niðrstigning*: on the times of sunrise and sunset.

fol. 14r, ch. 18   *Um borgaskipan oc legstaðe heilagra manna*: on the shrines and resting-places of saints.

As appears immediately, there is little attempt at any thematic grouping or logical ordering of the separate items: chs 1-4 and 7-8 are examples of medieval geography, notes on the location of places, rivers, peoples, monsters and marvels, compiled from a variety of familiar sources such as Isidore of Seville and *Elucidarius*.[20] Incidentally, the extracts

---

[20] On the sources see Þorkelsson, *Nökkur Blöð úr Hauksbók*. The chapters on monsters and marvels have no direct connection with the OE texts on the same subject in the *Beowulf* MS and in British Library, MS Cotton Tiberius B.5, which represent an earlier stage of

from *Elucidarius* (chs 10-13) do not correspond with the passages from *Elucidarius* translated into OE in MS G, which are the only extant portions of *Elucidarius* in OE: the OE and ON texts are apparently independent translations of extracts from the Latin original. Chapters 16-18 give further geographical information, but of a more practical kind such as might be useful to travellers, including sailors; the fact that the information in ch. 17 refers to Iceland indicates the provenance of that chapter, but it does not necessarily throw any light on the place of compilation of Hauksbók. The remaining chapters all contain religious material and several are concerned with paganism, idolatry and superstition. The chapters on these themes (5, 6, 9 and 10) draw heavily, if indirectly, on patristic writers, for some of whom paganism was a present or recent reality; it is impossible to say why these texts should have attracted the fourteenth-century copyist, but it is conceivable that they include material assembled at a much earlier date by someone who assumed that preaching in Norway might involve combating paganism. The title of ch. 9 is largely illegible but the seventeenth-century extracts from Hauksbók in MSS AM 281 4° and AM 597 4° give the title as *So s(eigir) S. Augustinus*, which agrees with the reference to Augustine at the beginning of the text:[21] this reference is taken over from Ælfric's *De auguriis*, the source of material in this chapter. Chapters 10-13 are from an ON version of *Elucidarius*, partly supplementing and partly overlapping with the version preserved later in Hauksbók.[22] The material on Ember Days and the rainbow (chs 14-15) is also preserved in other manuscripts.[23] In the unlikely context of this collection of oddments of conventional medieval learning there appears

the same tradition of writings: see James, *The Marvels of the East*, and Sisam, *Studies*, pp. 72-83.
[21] See Helgason, 'Til Hauksbóks historie'.
[22] See *H. edn*, pp. 470-99; the relationship of these texts is set out in *Elucidarius in Old Norse Translation*, ed. Firchow and Grimstad, which gives a full discussion and edition of all surviving texts.
[23] See Holtsmark, 'En gammel norsk homilie', and *Studier i Snorres Mytologi*, pp. 52-53, respectively.

the rarity with which we are concerned here, the only extant example of a sustained piece of translation from OE into ON; other texts in this section of Hauksbók that also depend in part on OE material are discussed below. The manuscript title, *Um þat hvaðan otru hofst*, 'how false belief arose', is appropriate to the first part of Ælfric's homily (P1-209) but not to the rest of the ON text, which is based on biblical stories of the conflict between Judaism and paganism, and it may be that this led the Hauksbók editors to assume that the title belonged to the first part only and that the rest must be a separate work requiring a new chapter-number.

THE OLD ENGLISH TEXT FROM WHICH THE TRANSLATION WAS MADE

Pope, followed by Taylor, mentions two points bearing on the question of the text used by the ON translator: first, the additional lines found in some manuscripts of Ælfric's homily, and secondly *Vena*, the peculiar form of the name Venus.

MSS R and S contain a passage not found in other manuscripts, P141-49 (mentioned above); since this passage does not appear in the translation, it could be inferred that the translator worked from a text of the CLW type, representing Ælfric's first version of the homily. Against this it must be acknowledged that there are other passages of comparable length omitted, apparently quite arbitrarily, from the translation (lines 11-47, 333-48, 725-43); such gaps in the extant translation suggest that the processes of translation, copying or abridgement could similarly account for the absence of P141-49 from the Hauksbók text even if the translator had used Ælfric's expanded RS version. Taylor asserts that the translator 'naturally omitted' these lines because they state that the Norse myths are mistaken if judged by the standards of classical paganism, but he does not explain why the translator should have wished to omit a specific charge against Norse paganism when he had chosen to translate a Christian homily that is a general attack on paganism.[24] The conclusion must be that the omission of the passage in question is merely negative evidence to which no great weight may be attached, though, for what it is worth, it points to the use of a manuscript of the CLW type.

The forms of the name Venus are more important and are the main basis of Taylor's view that R, or a manuscript like it, was used for the translation. The relevant facts are as follows: the name of Venus occurs in lines 226, 274 and 325 of Ælfric's *De falsis diis*; in nearly all the manuscripts containing these lines the name has the form *uenus* (usually

---

[24] Taylor, p. 103; the passage concerned, not in C, would fall between lines 212 and 213 below.

with a contraction for the final –*us*), but MS R is exceptional because in lines 274 and 325 it has the form *uena*, while at line 226 *uenus* seems to have been written over an original *uena*, or perhaps the reverse. In Hauksbók the forms vary: in 226 (H180) *venus* is superimposed over an original *vena*; at 274 (H219) the form *vena* is clear but a side-note in the margin, probably later, has *venus* (with –*us* contraction); at 325 (H253) the reading is unclear, but an original *venu* seems to have been changed to *veneri*, changing an ON dative case (of *Vena*) into a Latin dative case. The form *Vena* instead of *Venus* is thus confined to MS R and Hauksbók; MS S, which has much in common with R, breaks off at the beginning of line 274, so has the name at 226 only, where it has the normal form *uenus*. On the other hand, MS R inserts at line 274 an additional phrase found in no other manuscript of the homily: *uena on leden þæt is on denisc fricga* ('Venus in Latin, that is Frigg in Danish'); if this addition had been retained in Hauksbók the evidence would have been overwhelming, but it is not there. Pope further points out (p. 670) that in an eighth-century Latin homily cited by Levison the form *Venus* is taken to indicate the male sex.[25] Moreover (and, I would say, decisively), in line 223, where all manuscripts of the OE homily have the correct form of the name Juno (*iuno*), the ON text has the form *Iuna* (H177). The obvious inference is that among those with a limited knowledge of Latin grammar a simple belief that a –*us* inflection indicates masculine gender and –*a* indicates feminine gender might lead to some odd assumptions if applied dogmatically. As Pope rightly says, 'two persons of little Latin might have arrived at the same error', and the fact that a copyist (or conceivably even the original translator) quite independently 'regularised' Juno to *Iuna* shows that he was capable of

---

[25] See Levison, *England and the Continent*, pp. 302-14, Appendix I, 'Venus a man'; the text printed by Levison includes (p. 311) the sentence 'Et alia mulier fuit Iunae-Menerva meretrix . . . et fratres suos Martem et Venerem . . .' ('another woman was Juno's (?) Minerva, a harlot ... and her brothers Mars and Venus'): there was clearly a good deal of confusion in the early middle ages about the names and identities of pagan deities.

treating Venus in the same way. The evidence of *Vena*, pointing to the use of a manuscript like R, cannot be put aside, of course, but no great weight can be attached to it.

These two points then are both indecisive as well as conflicting: one points weakly to the use of a manuscript in the CLW tradition, the other no more strongly to the RS type. Other pieces of evidence are scarcely more decisive but it is worth summarising the arguments because in most cases the evidence, such as it is, points to the use of a text of the CLW type rather than RS.

> (1) Line 215: here CLWR all have *þrymlic*, 'glorious', but S has *þwyrlic*, 'perverse'; the latter is more appropriate in the context, but see Pope's note on his choice of the majority reading. The phrase *hetol* ('malevolent') *and þrymlic/þwyrlic* is translated in H168-69 as *illr oc grimr*, which would point to the use of a text like that in S if the translation were literal, but although there are instances of close verbal translation, approximate paraphrase is also common and there are no compelling grounds for assuming that this phrase belongs to one category rather than the other. The reading in Xk is interesting here: *hetol and grimlic and eac prymlic*, but this manuscript is too eccentric to be taken as representing a category that could have been available to the translator and there are no other unusual readings in it that coincide with anything in the ON text: the likeness of *grimlic* and *grimr* is probably a coincidence, the words are common in both languages as derogatory terms, but even if one wished to attach weight to it, its implication would be very unclear because of the unique nature of Xk.
>
> (2) Lines 225-26: S has uniquely *heora dohtra wæron gehaten Minerva and Venus*, where all other manuscripts omit *gehaten*; Hauksbók has *onnor het Minerva en onnor het Venus* and thus agrees with S in using a form of *hatan/heita*, but here again the translator is paraphrasing and it is difficult to see how he could have avoided *heita* in the syntax he had chosen.
>
> (3) A piece of evidence that Taylor claims points to the use of the RS version needs to be examined carefully. In lines 140-43 (P72-73) Pope's text reads *Nu ne ræde we on bocum þæt man arærde hæþengyld on eallum þam fyrste ær Noes flode*, 'now we do not read in the scriptures that anyone practised heathen worship in all the time before Noah's flood' (making the point that paganism only arose after the flood). As Pope points out,

the essential negative particle is omitted in RS but is included not only in CLW but also in Wulfstan's *De falsis diis*, an abridged adaptation of Ælfric's homily based on the revised RS version, so the negative must have been present in the authorial prototype of RS. The ON translation has *Sva segia oss heilagar bæcr at engi maðr skal blota heðnar vettir, firir þvi at þat gerðu menn firir Noa flod*, 'thus holy books tell us that no one may worship heathen spirits, because that is what men did before Noah's flood' (H93-96). Taylor claims that this 'makes it clear that it [the negative] was not in the translator's manuscript'. In fact it is not at all clear, for the Norse text here is a broad approximation that suggests that the translator had not clearly understood the original. The Norse text does in fact have the negative but transfers it from the main clause to the subordinate clause, apparently equating *nu ne ræde we on bocum þæt man* with *sva segia oss heilagar bæcr at engi maðr*, pointing to the use of an OE text with the negative. It is true that the further statement in the Norse text that idolatry was practised before the flood broadly agrees with the affirmative construction in RS ('we read in scripture that heathenism was practised'), but from *skal* onwards it looks as if the translator is extemporising on the basis of an only partially understood text (although one needs to be cautious over ascribing to the translator peculiarities that may have been introduced by a later reviser).

There is in fact no firm evidence pointing to the use of Ælfric's revised RS version: the occurrence of the name *Vena* is the only item that may be relevant, but it is far from conclusive.

Against this there are a few minor pointers in the opposite direction. The most important is that at lines 417-18, after the phrase *þa þa hi inn eoden*, C and L both add the words *to þam temple*, '(when they went in) to the temple', which are not in R; the translation has *er þeir komo inn i hof sitt* (H338), agreeing with CL. Less decisive, but pointing in the same direction, is the fact that the sentence following in line 420 has a present participle in R but an infinitive in C and L and also in the translation (R *licgende*, CL *licgan*, H340 *liggia*); normal ON syntax would probably favour the use of the infinitive rather than the participle here, so the point cannot carry much weight, but for what it is worth the correspondence is with CL. Of less significance is the fact that lines P314-17 (590-94 below) are preserved in CLG and in H but not in R; these lines are essential to the narrative and would not have been cut by Ælfric in the process of revision; one can only say that in this passage R is defective and the translation, which includes the relevant lines, was made from a non-defective text.

Within the CLW group the translation is at one point closer to L: in line 549 L uniquely inserts the name of the Babylonian king, which also appears in the translation. This point in favour of L needs to be seen in the light of the contradictory evidence of lines 858-63 (discussed below, p. 53, in connection with the translation of *leapas* as *laupa brauðs*); here L omits the word *leapas*, which the Norse text translates, but it also includes an addition (discussed below) that might have prompted the statement in the translation that the lions were starved for twelve days. At several other points L has individual peculiarities: these take the form of omissions in lines P215, P303 and P462, an addition in P356 and a variant in P350; none of these is reflected in the translation, which there agrees with C and R.

There is sadly little decisive evidence; the important factors, briefly summarised, are (i) favouring a text close to R, the occurrence of *Vena* in R and the translation; (ii) favouring a text close to C and L: the added phrase in 417-19 (P225), which is also in the translation. The latter probably outweighs the former. As between C and L, although L agrees with the translation in inserting the name of the king in 549, there are several cases where L is defective or exceptional, and in these the translation agrees with C (and incidentally with R). I have therefore taken C as the basis of the text printed below.

It must be emphasised that my concern here is not to print a text representing what Ælfric wrote: Pope's text, based on R, does this magisterially and renders further work unnecessary. My concern is rather to demonstrate the relationship between the OE and ON texts by printing an OE text as close as the manuscript evidence allows to that used by the translator. This purpose is best served by printing a text that is substantially that of C (omitting the final portion of the text in C for which there is no translation extant) and by substituting readings from other manuscripts where they are closer to the translation. MS C has the further advantage that it is closer in time to the translator: it is from the first half of the twelfth century and may be taken to represent the kind of manuscript that is most likely to have been accessible to the translator, who was probably at work in the twelfth century (see the discussion below). As shown above, C and L contain variants that are not in other manuscripts but which evidently underlie the translation, and L is also a twelfth-century manuscript. So too is S, which, in spite of its general closeness to R, also supplies two unique readings (at 215 and 225-26) that may have contributed to the ON translation. On the evidence of both historical proximity and textual minutiae, then, the translation is likely to have been made from a twelfth-century copy of Ælfric's homily, and of the manuscripts extant C is marginally closest to the text in Hauksbók. The main problem in discussing the translation is that while we have an OE text that must be fairly close to that used by the translator, the ON text in H must be at some distance from the original version produced by the translator and is in places the result of fairly drastic rewriting.

If we accept Pope's arguments that R comes closest to Ælfric's final version (and the arguments are compelling), then it is broadly true that unauthorised variants increase among the extant manuscripts as they become remoter from Ælfric's own time; this is not surprising in texts that were subject to fairly frequent copying, but in practice it partly contradicts the concept of two families of manuscripts, one (CLW) deriving from an original version, the other from a revised version (RS). Of course, Pope does not propose any such rigid theory and he makes it clear that his theory of revision involves nothing more than the addition of one short passage (P141-49); as regards these lines, and also the omission of the negative in 140 (P72), R and S form a group apart, but not in other respects. Setting aside this added passage, and also the incompleteness of GSW, and to a lesser extent L, one can make two points about the manuscripts of *De falsis diis*: first, the differences between them are not great and (apart from the added P141-49) do not indicate any substantial changes at any point; and second, what differences there are are not distributed so systematically as to indicate clear families of manuscripts. Although there are cases where the distribution of readings supports the distinction of RS from CLW (the omission of the negative in 140 or the added phrase in 417-18), there is no case apart from P141-49 where a difference in reading can be ascribed to authorial revision. Moreover, there are cases where the distribution of readings cuts across this division, so that CLR agree against S (215 and 225). Each manuscript offers its own version of the text and no stemma can be devised, but the differences are only in minor details. One can say that the translator worked from a text of *De falsis diis* that contained some readings peculiar to twelfth-century copies of the homily but did not correspond exactly to any one extant manuscript.

THE DATE AND PROVENANCE OF THE OLD NORSE TRANSLATION OF *DE FALSIS DIIS*

It is impossible to establish the place and date of the translation with anything approaching certainty. As regards date, the only certain *termini* are the composition of Ælfric's homily in the years around 1000 and the copying of the text into Hauksbók in the early fourteenth century, while the translation could have been made in England or Scandinavia (including Iceland), but these wide uncertainties can be reduced somewhat.

First, the place: the ON text is preserved in a portion of the manuscript that may have been copied by a Norwegian: *H. fac.* identifies the copyist as 'the first Norwegian hand' and a Norwegian connection is supported by the fact, discussed more fully below, that the translation seems to have contributed a minor detail in an early stage of the sagas of St Olaf. It might therefore seem reasonable to assume that the translation was made in Norway; indeed, this was my own initial assumption, though it is hard to reconcile with what is known about the circulation of Ælfric manuscripts in OE.

Regarding the date, an initial assumption must be that the eleventh and twelfth centuries were the period when Ælfric's homilies were valued highly enough to merit transcription and adaptation and hence, possibly, translation, and furthermore an OE original can hardly have been used much after about 1200 in any location on grounds of comprehensibility; if the *Legendary Saga of St Olaf* borrowed from the ON *De falsis diis*, this would also support a *terminus ante quem* about 1200 for the completion of the translation. It is tempting to ascribe the translation to the earliest phase (late eleventh or early twelfth century) of vernacular writing in Norway and Iceland (as described, for example, by Turville-Petre and Bekker Nielsen), but there is no obvious evidence in favour of this.[26] A somewhat later date in the second half

---

[26] Turville-Petre, *Origins,* pp. 109-42, and Bekker-Nielsen, 'Frode mænd og tradition', pp. 35-41.

of the twelfth century might be supported by the fact (discussed further below) that there are passages that the translator may not fully have understood. The subsequent process of copying the translated text in Norway presumably eliminated any linguistic clues as to the date of translation, as well as any evidence as to the native language of the translator.

Both date and location may however be illuminated by a more detailed consideration of fundamental aspects of the work and one can find pointers to a milieu in which the translation may have been undertaken.

For the translation of a substantial learned prose-text such as this from OE into ON there are certain prerequisites, and it is helpful to spell these out in detail. The first of these is access to the original English text, the second is an ability to read and understand this text, the third is an ability to render the sense of the original OE in ON, and the fourth is an ability to transcribe this new version into writing. These prerequisites raise questions but also point to possible solutions.

First, access to a copy of Ælfric's text: here the evidence points firmly to England: England is the obvious place in which to find manuscripts of a work in OE and there is no evidence for the presence of manuscripts of Ælfric's homilies in Norway, or even for the presence there of any English-language manuscripts. It may sound reasonable to postulate that an English churchman visiting Norway might take such a text with him, but there is no known example of this kind of behaviour and there is no evidence for the private ownership of manuscripts (other than biblical and liturgical) among the lower clergy at this period. More plausibly, a copy of Ælfric's writings might have been sent to a Norwegian religious house, particularly to one founded from England, but it is hard to see what use could have been envisaged for texts in English. Latin manuscripts are of course a different matter and there is abundant evidence for the circulation in Norway of Latin liturgical manuscripts from England, but not of manuscripts in English.[27] This first prerequisite, together with everything known about the circulation of OE manuscripts, thus favours the possibility that the translation was made in England at a religious house that held a copy of Ælfric's *De falsis diis*.

The second prerequisite, literacy in English, is less informative: Englishmen literate in their own language were obviously to be found in England and could well have travelled abroad. English churchmen who undertook evangelisation in Norway presumably had some degree of literacy in Latin, and may have been literate in English too, but not necessarily: literacy in English is virtually certain for the late Anglo-Saxon period, but less certain in the twelfth century when the translation is likely to have been made, for in England the conquest was followed by an increase in clergy who had apparently not been trained in the late OE scribal tradition. I know of no information about literacy in English among Scandinavian churchmen, but it is in any case obvious that anyone able to read and interpret an OE text is more likely to have been found in England than anywhere else.

The third prerequisite, knowledge of the two languages, was probably reasonably widespread but perhaps haphazard: there are always individuals capable of learning a foreign language and, more importantly, there was apparently a Norse-speaking element in the population of England foll-

---

[27] On liturgical manuscripts of English origin in Norway see Abrams, 'Eleventh-century missions', p. 26, and Abrams, 'Christianisation', pp. 245-46. A representative example is Oslo, Riksarkivet, MS Lat. fr. 145, Kalendarium, s.xii in., originally from Crowland Abbey, Lincolnshire. See also Abram, 'Scandinavian context'. Gneuss, *Handlist*, p. 134, lists several Latin manuscripts of English origin in Oslo, Riksarkivet, but gives no information about how long they have been in Norway: many are probably early imports. See further Corrêa, 'A mass for St Birinus'. One may also note that the Copenhagen Ælfric fragments (originally part of *Ker* 118: see *CH* 1, pp. 56-59) probably arrived in Denmark in the post-medieval period (seventeenth century?); *Ker* 99, a Wulfstan MS that probably reached Denmark soon after compilation, is mainly (though not completely) in Latin: see *The Copenhagen Wulfstan Collection*, ed. Cross and Tunberg, and Gerritsen, 'The Copenhagen Wulfstan Manuscript'.

owing the Scandinavian settlements of the ninth and early tenth centuries in the East Midlands and the North, in an area that is conventionally delineated by the presence of place-names of ON origin and by the survival of ON elements in Middle English dialects. The later conquest of England by Svein and Cnut led to the superimposition of a Danish aristocracy over a much wider area in the early eleventh century, resulting in a Danish-language presence that, on the evidence of place-names and Middle English dialects, was less intensive than that resulting from earlier settlements, but was more widespread, certainly not restricted to areas of previous settlement in the Danelaw; Danish language competence in this connection may have been, under Cnut and his sons, more socially distinguished, in some sense official or aristocratic or, at any rate, associated with the royal court.[28] For the present purpose there is no need to distinguish between the different varieties of ON that subsequently gave rise to the later Scandinavian languages: whatever variety there may have been among speakers of different national origins, the tendency in England was to group them all together as 'heathens' or 'Danes', while Scandinavians seem to have referred to all versions of their own language as *á Danska tungu*, as in *De falsis diis*, H193; cf. H218, *a donsku;* and most famously in the opening sentence of Snorri's Prologue to *Heimskringla* (where the Norwegian kings who are the subject of the history are said to have spoken *á danska tungu;* see further Fritzner, *Ordbog,* s.v. *danskr*); linguistic variety among native speakers of ON before the twelfth century was apparently no impediment to communication. It is therefore irrelevant whether the translator of *De falsis diis* might trace his descent or his linguistic knowledge to one part of Scandinavia rather than another.

---

[28] These issues are briefly discussed with fuller references in Frankis, 'Sidelights on post-conquest Canterbury' (esp. pp. 14-17). For important recent studies that somewhat modify earlier views see Hadley, 'Cockle amongst the wheat'; Hadley, 'Viking and native'; Townend, 'Viking Age England'; and, most comprehensively, Townend, *Language and History.* See also studies listed in n. 30.

There is firm evidence for the presence of speakers of some form of Scandinavian language in many parts of England at least to the middle of the eleventh century, and there are a few pointers to the survival in post-conquest England of a distinct Scandinavian ('Danish') element in the population. A few years after the conquest (before 1070) a writ of king William guarantees the authority of the abbot and abbey of Bury St Edmunds over part of Suffolk, against any rival claim to control by anyone else, 'English, French or Danish' (*æðer ge Engliscan ge Frenkiscan ge Denniscan*). The reference to French and English elements of the population is of course a recurrent formula in post-conquest documents, but the inclusion here of Danish as a third element of apparently the same kind, specifically in East Anglia, is particularly striking. It is difficult to be sure what distinguished these groups (clothing, manners, appearance may all have contributed), but language is surely the most likely factor. More than a century later a Devonshire diploma (1174-84) is witnessed by, among others, a William *Dacus* (a Latin formulation for 'Dane', like *Dacia* for 'Denmark', common among twelfth-century Latin writers like William of Newburgh and Walter Map), who is also referred to as *le Deneys*: he could conceivably, if perhaps improbably, have been a recent immigrant, but while the name William was very common in England it was apparently still rare in Denmark at that date, so a man presumably born in England by the mid-twelfth century was in this case named for his distinctive ancestry.[29]

A form of Scandinavian language was presumably spoken in England at least to the end of the eleventh century but evidence for literary activity in such a language in England is limited and, such as it is, points in all probability to oral

---

[29] Pelteret, *Catalogue*, pp. 58 (no. 19) and 85 (no. 58). Hald, *Personnavne*, makes no mention of any form of *Wilhelm / William* about this time.

composition, particularly of skaldic verse and, less decisively, eddic poems, in the tenth and earlier eleventh centuries.[30]

As regards writing in ON, the fourth prerequisite listed above, the contrast between the status of English and Norse has been set out clearly by Matthew Townend: 'there is effectively no evidence whatsoever for the writing of ON in England in any other alphabet than the runic, and one can readily observe at Cnut's court a sharp distinction between spoken Norse and written English (and Latin).'[31] This is no doubt true, especially if one is thinking of sustained prose-composition, but it does not quite address the problem of the rise of Norse literacy and the use of the Latin alphabet for recording Scandinavian languages. The dating of this phenomenon is uncertain, but the earliest surviving manuscripts in a Scandinavian language are all from twelfth-century Scandinavia.[32] The writing of ON in runic script had of course been practised for many hundreds of years, and though the transition from runes to the Latin alphabet was probably neither simple nor automatic, the history of runic writing may possibly cast a little light on the matter. The expansion of the ON shorter futhark probably took place under the influence of contacts with the Latin alphabet, and it has been authoritatively argued that this occurred in

---

[30] Frank, 'King Cnut', esp. pp. 108-10; McKinnell, 'The context of *Völundarkviða*'. For further discussion of these matters see Fellows-Jensen, 'In the steps of the Vikings'; Parsons, 'Scandinavian language'; Jesch, 'Skaldic verse'; and McKinnell, 'Eddic poetry': all in Graham-Campbell et al., eds, *Vikings and the Danelaw*; Townend, 'Contextualizing the *Knútsdrápur*'. See also Bjork, 'Scandinavian relations'. These studies are mainly centred in the pre-conquest period, especially the tenth and earlier eleventh centuries and (excepting that by Parsons) have less to say about the continued use of Scandinavian language(s) in England in the later eleventh and twelfth, but Jesch's comments ('Skaldic verse', pp. 321-22) on one skaldic verse from 1076 are particularly valuable.

[31] Townend, 'Viking Age England', p. 95, further amplified in Townend, *Language and History*, pp. 189-96.

[32] The basic facts are set out in Haugen, *The Scandinavian Languages*, pp. 185-86 and 194-95; see also Noreen, *Altisländische Grammatik*, pp. 21-26 (para. 15.B); also the works cited in n. 26.

England rather than in Scandinavia.[33] There is also the further fact that the earliest known ON inscriptions in the Latin alphabet (leaving aside names recorded by chroniclers writing in Latin or English) are on coins minted in the first half of the tenth century for Scandinavian kings in England, which include not only names but at least one recurrent word, CVNVNC and CVNVNG (for ON *konungr*).[34] This use of ON in the Latin alphabet is all the more remarkable in view of the fact that English coins of the period, which presumably served as models, generally used Latin for any text added to the king's name ('Eadmund rex' is a typical example), and it shows that experiments in the use of the Latin alphabet for recording ON words not only go back far beyond the earliest extant manuscripts but are also crucially first attested in England. However, it is curious that coins minted in Scandinavia for Cnut in the first half of the eleventh century, although they offer complex problems of interpretation, apparently show no advance in the adoption of the Latin alphabet for ON inscriptions: rather the contrary, in fact, for moneyers, some of whom had English names, use either Latin (CNVT REX IN DAN) or English (ON LVN, 'in Lund', and ON ROSCEL, 'in Roskilde'), presumably because they did not know any system for representing ON (Danish) with the Latin alphabet.[35] One might conclude that before the mid-eleventh century there is fragmentary evidence for the use of the Latin alphabet for writing of ON in England but none in Scandinavia. This suggests that it is extremely unlikely that there could have been any attempt to write a continuous ON text, or to translate a written text from OE to ON, in the reign of Cnut and his sons (before, that is, the mid-eleventh century).

---

[33] See Page and Hagland, 'Runica manuscripta', p. 68.
[34] For examples see Roesdahl et al., eds, *The Vikings in England*, pp. 103 (G38, dated 940), 135 (YTC42-4, dated 939-40 and 943-44), 140 (ill.*h*, dated 939-40, ONLAF CVNVNC) and 145 (bottom row left, dated 941-43, ANLAF CVNVNG); Blunt, Stewart and Lyon, *Coinage in Tenth Century England*, pp. 211-34; also discussed by Townend, *Language and History*, pp. 195-96.
[35] See Jonsson, 'The coinage of Cnut', pp. 223-30 and Fig. 11.8.

This still leaves much unclear concerning the origins of ON literacy using the Latin alphabet and the subsequent development of the written literary tradition that presumably lies behind the ON *De falsis diis*; but, as is well known, English handwriting was an important model for the script adopted in Norway (and, to a lesser extent, in Iceland); it has also been shown that the ON tradition of homiletic composition had its beginnings in England. The adoption into ON of English loanwords referring to writing and parchment attests to oral contacts, but the adoption of the literary phrase *guðs dyrlingr* (from OE *godes dyrling*) may attest to the reading and imitating of OE religious texts by some Scandinavians, presumably in England.[36] It has long been recognised that English missionaries in Norway were influential in the rise and spread of the use of the Latin alphabet for recording ON, but it seems that this process began in England. Dating the whole process remains problematic: its origins may have been in the first half of the tenth century on coins minted in England, but fully developed literacy involving manuscripts probably arose during the late eleventh and early twelfth centuries, the great period of English missionary activity in Scandinavia.

The devising of a system of writing for ON, at least partially modelled on an existing system for English, implies the existence of a community in which there was some degree of both bilingualism and literacy, and such a community, presumably in England, is a possible milieu for the making of the ON translation of *De falsis diis*. The

---

[36] Relevant palaeographical facts are summarised by Turville-Petre, *Origins*, pp. 74-76 (where the emphasis is on Iceland), and by Ole Widding, 'Skriften', where references to Iceland are supplemented with a passage on Norway (pp. 29-30); see also Haugen, *Scandinavian Languages*, pp. 194-98, and references on p. 244; and Gunnlaugsson, 'Manuscripts and palaeography', pp. 246-48 and 255-57. An English origin for Norse homiletic composition is proposed by Gatch, 'The achievement of Ælfric', p. 55; further amplified by Abram, 'Scandinavian context'. On linguistic adoptions see Turville-Petre, *Origins*, p. 75; *godes dyrling*: several examples in Ælfric (e.g. *Pope* I. 230: 2.5), frequent in post-conquest writing; *guðs dyrlingr*: *Gamal norsk homiliebok*, p. 108 (lines 30-31).

translator was presumably a cleric resident in England (probably, but not necessarily, an English speaker with Scandinavian connections, perhaps descended from immigrants from the time of Cnut, since such a man might have been exposed to a bilingual background) who intended that a copy of his translation should be taken to Scandinavia, most probably to Norway, for use by clerics there; he was presumably a monk, since a monk is the most likely person to have had access to an Ælfric manuscript. Alternatively, the translator could conceivably have been a Scandinavian cleric visiting an English monastery who saw a use for such a text in his home-country, but in that case one would probably need to postulate some degree of guidance from an English cleric on the choice of a text, and perhaps collaboration in the task, so that further hypotheses begin to proliferate. The translation must have been made at a time when the homilies of Ælfric were still understood and valued, which could hardly have been much later than 1200. Manuscripts of Ælfric's homilies continued to be copied in English monasteries throughout the twelfth century, but by the thirteenth century the language began to present problems of comprehension, as appears in the work of the famous 'tremulous hand' of Worcester, a monk active in the first half of the thirteenth century in a linguistically conservative area, who evidently attempted, with some difficulties, to read OE texts and wrote glosses, mainly in Latin, as part of his study. The place in which the translation of *De falsis diis* is most likely to have been made is one of the English monasteries in which Anglo-Saxon religious texts were copied and adapted for new purposes in the post-conquest period, especially in the twelfth century, as described in recent studies by Elaine Treharne and others. In centres where OE texts were being adapted for a later English readership, the further step of translating some of them for readers unfamiliar with English is exemplified in the Latin translation of the *Anglo-Saxon Chronicle* in BL MS Cotton Domitian A.viii (made at Canterbury Cathedral around 1100) and in William of Malmesbury's *Vita Wulfstani* (from an OE original, early twelfth century); the activity of translation from OE into ON could well have found a place in the general milieu in which Anglo-Saxon literary and historical traditions became a source and stimulus for writing in French, as described by Elizabeth Tyler.[37]

How the idea of translating an English text into ON arose is unknowable, but translation specifically from OE appears in the post-conquest period both in the Latin versions of the *Anglo-Saxon Chronicle* and the *Vita Wulfstani*, and in the adaptation into French (Anglo-Norman) of parts of the *Anglo-Saxon Chronicle* in Gaimar's *Estoire des Engleis* (1136-37), and this activity may have been a model for translation from OE into ON; but in any case, the translator must have been familiar with some tradition of writing ON, which could hardly have been before 1100 and was probably rather later. There are in any case two opposed tendencies: on one hand, the necessary linguistic knowledge and the access, both physical and intellectual, to the original OE text are best explained by postulating an early date for the translation; on the other hand, the requirement for some kind of tradition of writing in ON is best met by a later date. All things considered, some time in the twelfth century, probably in the second half, is the most likely date for the making of the translation.

Copies of Anglo-Saxon homilies continued to be produced in several monastic scriptoria throughout the twelfth century, and there is no evidence for the preservation and circulation of such material outside a monastic milieu, so one can probably assume that the Norse translation of *De falsis diis* was made in an English religious house that maintained a library of Anglo-Saxon texts, especially homilies, and

---

[37] See Franzen, *The Tremulous Hand of Worcester*; on the problems that one English scribe had copying OE homilies c.1200 see Swan, 'Preaching past the Conquest'. Translations from OE: *The Anglo-Saxon Chronicle*, ed. Baker; *Vita Wulfstani*: see Proud, 'Old English prose saints' lives', p. 117. Tyler, 'From Old English to Old French'. For one example of language-contact in an Ælfric manuscript, MS L, see Frankis, 'Languages and cultures in contact'.

encouraged the copying and adaptation of them.[38] The important centres of such activity were the cathedral priories of Canterbury, Rochester, Winchester, Worcester and Durham, and some other pre-conquest Benedictine foundations; these were mostly not in areas of earlier Scandinavian settlement, but individuals with a knowledge of both languages were not confined to the Danelaw, and Danish immigrants from the time of Cnut were to be found over much of England; even in Canterbury, a place with no obvious Scandinavian connections, a Norse runic charm was copied into a post-conquest Anglo-Saxon manuscript.[39] Monasteries that had contacts with Scandinavia included the Benedictine abbeys of Evesham and Abingdon,[40] and the Abbey of Bury St Edmunds in Suffolk was host to Eysteinn, Archbishop of Trondheim, during his exile in 1181-82 when he may have been working on his Latin life of St Olaf.[41] Coincidentally, the Abbey of Bury St Edmunds, traditionally believed to have been refounded by Cnut to commemorate the ninth-century martyr killed by Danish invaders, held in the thirteenth century a manuscript (now British Library, MS Cotton Julius E.vii: MS W) that contains a text of *De falsis diis* and which may have been there at the time of Eysteinn's visit; but the library of Bury St Edmunds, to judge from what survives, held very little in the way of manuscripts

---

[38] The continued post-conquest copying and adaptation of Anglo-Saxon texts is discussed throughout Swan and Treharne, *Rewriting Old English*; see also Treharne, 'English in the post-conquest period'.

[39] The implications of this are discussed in Frankis, 'Sidelights on post-conquest Canterbury', pp. 14-17. Townend, 'Contextualizing the *Knútsdrápur*' (n. 30 above), plausibly argues for Danish language activity at the royal court in Winchester in the reign of Cnut, but this is unlikely to have survived the death of Cnut and his sons.

[40] The Evesham link with Odense in Denmark is presumably not relevant to a work that ended up in Norway (and ultimately in Iceland), but see King, 'The cathedral priory of Odense'; the Abingdon link with Norway may be relevant but whether Abingdon Abbey was a likely location for any activity involving translation must remain uncertain: see Graham, 'A runic entry'.

[41] Jocelin of Brakelond, *Chronicle of Bury St Edmunds*, trans. Greenway and Sayers, pp. 15 and 128; discussions of Eysteinn are summarised in *A History of Norway*, trans. Kunin, pp. xxx-xxxi.

in OE and the monks there apparently did not share in the antiquarian interests that led to the copying and adaptation of OE texts in some other Benedictine houses in the twelfth century.[42] Whatever writing on St Olaf Archbishop Eysteinn may have done at Bury St Edmunds, the *Passio et miracula beati Olaui* makes no mention of the particular motif from *De falsis diis* discussed below, so this connection must remain of dubious relevance.

For the location of the translation there are thus several possibilities, with varying degrees of likelihood, but a precise place is impossible to identify. In any case, a monastic context, suggested by Ælfric's opening invocation, *gebroðra þa leofostan*, is supported by its retention in the translation, *liufir brœðr*: original and translation are both addressed to a clerical, even monastic, readership or audience.

A further relevant factor (discussed in more detail below) is that the portion of Hauksbók that contains the translation of *De falsis diis* also contains another text, *Heimslýsing* ch. 9, that shows some use of another work by Ælfric, the homily *De auguriis*. Wherever the translation of *De falsis diis* was made, we should probably postulate that the precursor of the ON text based on *De auguriis* was made at the same time in the same place, and both were eventually taken to Norway, presumably together since they ended up together. How far this situation is clarified by a third OE text for which an ON translation is extant, the *Prose Phoenix*, is also discussed below.

One can thus make reasonably well founded conjectures about the milieu in which the translation was made, but the milieu in which it subsequently circulated is more elusive, though there are numerous ON writings from the twelfth and thirteenth centuries that share in varying forms the same

---

[42] MS W described above, and see *Pope* I, 83-85; for manuscripts at Bury see Ker, *Medieval Libraries*, pp. 16-22. See further Thomson, 'The Library of Bury St Edmunds Abbey'; Proud, 'Old English prose saints' lives', p. 121, n. 20, notes that MS W 'shows no signs of twelfth-century use'. The role that Abram, 'Scandinavian context', pp. 443-44, wishes to ascribe to Bury might be difficult to substantiate.

interest in a Christian approach to the pagan gods of Scandinavia.

There is no reason to believe that the translation was made for inclusion in anything like its present setting: the texts in *Heimslýsing* were gathered together from a variety of sources and their arrangement does not throw any obvious light on the nature of these sources. Nor should it be assumed that the translation was made for a society in which paganism was still a serious menace: like the original OE homily it belongs to an established tradition of preaching that was only partly modified to take account of the realities of the preacher's own society. Denunciations of superstition were no doubt relevant to all European societies in the middle ages, and it had early become a point of preaching technique to link them with the theme of paganism. *Heimslýsing* contains various texts on superstition and paganism (the extracts from *De falsis diis*, *De auguriis* and *Elucidarius*) and it is probable that the collector (perhaps the scribe, perhaps Haukr himself) was motivated by something like the antiquarian interest that finds expression in the prologue to Snorri's *Edda* and parts of Saxo's *Gesta Danorum*.[43] Saxo's account of Starkatherus includes a digression on pagan gods and the names of the days of the week;[44] this theme occurs of course in *De falsis diis*, 305-32, and in its source in Martin of Braga's *De correctione rusticorum*, ch. 8, but it also appears in several twelfth-century works, including Geoffrey of Monmouth's *Historia regum Britanniae*, VI. 98, and William of

---

[43] Jakobsson, 'Hauksbók', suggests that Hauksbók was planned by Haukr himself and reflects his antiquarian interests. See also U. and P. Dronke, 'The Prologue of the Prose *Edda*'. *Saxonis gesta Danorum*, ed. Olrik and Ræder, I. vii. 1 and VI. v. 3-5. On the Scandinavian revival of interest in paganism see Abram, *Myths*, pp. 193-208.

[44] *Gesta Danorum* V. 2-6, p. 152; *Saxo Grammaticus*, ed. Davidson, I. 170-71, with commentary in II. 99-100.

Malmesbury's *Gesta regum Angliae*.⁴⁵ The interests of the compiler of *Heimslýsing* were thus of a kind that had been widely current for some time, not only at the time when the translation was being made and copied. The same interests not infrequently appear in Icelandic literature, most strikingly in *Barlaams Saga*, where an account of euhemerism and the origins of paganism after the flood is followed by an account of the Greek pagan gods and the story of Dagon and the Ark of the Covenant and a further denunciation of classical paganism; there is even a story about Gregory Thaumaturgus that had been included in Ælfric's *De falsis diis* (P572-648).⁴⁶ Whether this sequence of themes in *Barlaams saga* was influenced by a knowledge of the ON *De falsis diis* is uncertain: there are no close verbal echoes and the material could have been assembled independently from a range of sources, including some of those used by Ælfric, and it may illustrate nothing more than a community of interest in the Scandinavian world in the twelfth and thirteenth centuries, though obviously influence from *De falsis diis* cannot be excluded. Broadly similar references to paganism, in which source-references to classical deities are rendered in terms of Norse gods and goddesses, are by no means uncommon in Icelandic and Norse writing, appearing in texts as diverse as the ON *Elucidarius* and several saints' lives, *Clemens saga* being notable for a strikingly detailed list of Norse pagan gods.⁴⁷

---

⁴⁵ Also in OE writing in *Byrhtferth's Enchiridion*, ed. Baker and Lapidge, pp. 28 and 118 (I.2.89 and II.3.217); Geoffrey of Monmouth, *The History of the Kings of Britain*, ed. Reeve, pp. 124-25, 275-83; *De gestis regum Anglorum*, ed. and trans. Mynors et al., I.5.3, and notes in II. 20. On the names of the days of the week in general see Green, *Language and History*, pp. 236-53.

⁴⁶ *Barlaams ok Josaphats Saga*, ed. Keyser and Unger, chs 30, 138, 168-69 and 65: pp. 24-26, 134-38, 166-68 and 63-67.

⁴⁷ *The Old Norse Elucidarius*, ed. Firchow, p. 70; for *Clemens saga* see *Postola Sögur*, ed. Unger, pp. xv-xvii and 146-47; later studies of this passage are listed in *Clemens Saga*, ed. and trans. Carron, pp. xxi-xxii. On the evidence for an Anglo-Scandinavian cult of St Clement see Crawford, 'The St Clement dedications'.

This widespread revival of interest in Norse paganism may well have been influential in the preservation and circulation of the ON *De falsis diis* following its presumed arrival in Norway, but is of less relevance to the other ON texts translated from OE.

THE OLD ENGLISH AND OLD NORSE TEXTS OF *DE FALSIS DIIS*

In view of the long time-lapse between the making of the original translation, presumably well before 1200, and the transcription of the extant text, after 1300, it is difficult to say much with certainty about the translator's method: there was ample time for many kinds of changes to take place, whether accidental mistakes in the process of copying or deliberate rewriting of the work. Where the ON text is close to the OE original it presumably represents the translator's work but departures from the original may be due either to the translator or to subsequent revision. One clearly need not hold the translator responsible for all omissions, additions and other changes of the original, and many linguistic details of the original translation must presumably have been fairly drastically modernised in the process of copying. Nevertheless, when the various kinds of change are analysed it is occasionally possible to make a tentative distinction between the work of the translator and that of subsequent revisers.

(a) The portions of the Old English text omitted from the translation

The chief omissons are lines 11-47, 98-113, 180-193, 333-48, 506-13, 725-43, 755-62 and 931 to the end. The omission of lines 11-47, 180-93 and 333-48 is probably due to difficulties in the subject matter of these passages: the nature of the Trinity (11-47: further references to the Trinity in 48-53 are also omitted), the question of divine permission (180-93), and the obscurity of Ælfric's account of the movement of the planets (333-48: see Pope's note on P181-86). The translator was evidently unable or unwilling to discuss theological and intellectual subtleties, perhaps because his knowledge of ON did not extend to such subjects. There is no obvious explanation for the omission of 725-43 and 755-62, and in fact the translation of the whole passage (664-800) is seriously impaired by the lack of these lines: in 725-54 Ælfric, following his biblical source, poses the problem of access to the locked temple, and in 755-63 he gives the solution in the account of the underground passageway. Because of the omission of both of these passages the ON version here leaves the problem of entry into the locked temple unexplained; this may have been due to a fault in translation, but a later omission in copying is equally possible.

The omission of P141-49 has been mentioned above (pp. 7-8) as it is a point of textual significance, while the omission of the closing section of the homily (see p. 15) is likely to be due to later abridgement: evidence that this section was originally translated is presented below and the extant version of the ON text probably results from deliberate abridgement of a kind found in other texts in Hauksbók, reflecting an editorial policy.[48]

This leaves several minor omissions (451-56, 458, 477-78 and 506-13), which reflect a systematic exclusion from the translation of all references in the original to the five towns of the Philistines (enumerated in 1 Samuel 6.17 but not listed by name in Ælfric's text). It may be that the translator did not understand the reference and so left it out, but another possibility arises when one considers the implications that this theme may have had for Ælfric. In telling the story of Dagon and the Ark of the Covenant (lines 396-532) Ælfric repeatedly refers to the five towns of the Philistines as *fíf burga* (lines 454, 458, 477-8 and 509); this phrase of course occurs frequently in Old English records, including the *Anglo-Saxon Chronicle* and Æthelred's law-code given at Wantage, to refer to the five towns of the Danelaw (Lincoln, Derby, Nottingham, Leicester and Stanford).[49] Ælfric's repetition of the phrase *fíf burga* is so insistent as to suggest

---

[48] See *H. fac.*, introduction; I am indebted to Professor Hans Bekker-Nielsen for this suggestion.

[49] *Two Saxon Chronicles*, ed. Earle, pp. 110 and 146: MS A, *sub anno* 942 (in a poem celebrating the liberation of the five towns from Norse domination) and 1015, both contexts emphasising the separateness of the five towns from the kingdom of Wessex; also from the latter period, in the law-code given by Æthelræd at Wantage: see Liebermann, *Die Gesetze der Angelsachsen*, I.228 (1, 1).

that he wishes to make a comparison between the five towns of the Philistines and the five towns of the Danelaw, implying that the Danelaw was a stronghold of paganism, Philistia to the Israel of Wessex. Such an implication doubtless raises historical questions: there is no evidence for any survival of paganism in the mid-tenth century in the district of the five towns, or indeed anywhere else among established Scandinavian immigrants, and well before Ælfric's time there had been several leading churchmen of (at least in part) Danish descent, including an archbishop of Canterbury,[50] but Ælfric may rather have wished to suggest that there had been a revival or reimposition of paganism in the Danelaw as a result of the late tenth-century invasion. Such an implication would accord with the well-documented anti-Danish sentiments widespread in southern England in Ælfric's lifetime, as mentioned above.[51] Perhaps Ælfric knew of the Wantage law-code, which affirms that the laws of Wessex did not apply in the five towns, and he took this to imply (perhaps wrongly, though the distinction between religious law and civil law may not have been fully clarified then) that there was some rivalry to Christian religion in that area; in another homily (*Pope* II. 521: XIV. 132-39 and note) Ælfric even says that Englishmen who submit to the 'Danes' (the generic term for all Scandinavians) are alienating themselves from God and his saints and acting against their Lord. In this part of *De falsis diis* Ælfric implies a parallel between Danes and Philistines, and it is then possible that the translator was aware of this implication and wished to reject it by omitting all references to the five towns; this would depend on his having some knowledge of English geography and of the history of the tenth and eleventh centuries, perhaps even some kind of national or local pride. Such knowledge and

---

[50] Oda, archbishop of Canterbury (941-58) and his relatives Oscytel, archbishop of York (956-71) and Oswald, bishop of Worcester (961-92) and archbishop of York 971-92, the last being one of the leaders of the tenth-century reform movement; details are summarised by Abrams, 'The conversion of the Danelaw', p. 37 and n. 14.

[51] See n. 11 above. Relevant evidence is presented by Townend, *Language and History*, pp. 135-38.

attitudes could hardly be expected in a native Scandinavian, but might plausibly be found in someone brought up in a part of England where an element of the population was aware of its Scandinavian ancestry and was anxious to repudiate any suggestion that this involved any failing in Christian orthodoxy. The existence in post-conquest England of some kind of pro-Danish sympathy seems in fact to be implicit in the reference in the *Anglo-Saxon Chronicle* to the murder of the Danish king St Knut (MS E *sub anno* 1086: this portion of the Chronicle is generally held to be of early twelfth-century origin, so may represent a view current only a little earlier than the translation of *De falsis diis*); the passage concerned refers to *þa Dænescan þe wæs ærur geteald eallra folca getreowast*, 'the Danes, who were formerly reckoned to be the most trustworthy of all people'.[52] This whole argument about the five towns, based on negative evidence, is obviously tenuous, but a satisfactory explanation for these omissions is hard to find: some of the other omissions seem to be unmotivated, but there is none so highly selective as this systematic exclusion of a repeated phrase.

The omissions from the translation are thus somewhat inconclusive as regards the motivation and identity of the translator, but suggest a reluctance to write on matters of intellectual subtlety and perhaps point to the possibilty that he may have been an English resident of Scandinavian descent.

(b) The treatment of the portions translated

The translator's method varies from close, almost word for word, translation (for example, 150-59, 410-22, 514-18) to loose paraphrase, paraphrase being commoner than literal translation, particularly in the latter part of the homily, though there it may be due to the work of a reviser. An example of free translation is at 397, where a reference to the

---

[52] *Two Saxon Chronicles*, I.221: the whole entry is in rough alliterative verse.

sins of the Israelites is translated as *syndum þeira hinna cristna manna*, 'sins of the Christian people'; the translator may have been careless or he may have had a didactic intention, showing the audience how they should interpret Old Testament stories.

Perhaps the most obvious feature of the translation however is its frequent inaccuracy. The misunderstandings are often trivial, and in some cases the translator's mental processes can be conjectured with reasonable confidence: an example is at 207, where OE *þa þa*, 'when', was evidently taken as an equivalent of the ON relative construction *þá er*, 'those who', and translated as *hverrn sem*, 'each one who' (or 'each as'); this equating of similar forms need not have any bearing on the native language of the translator, but is perhaps more suggestive of a native speaker of a form of ON. In other cases the mistake is more puzzling, as at 176 (H148, emended), where *eigi* is apparently arbitrarily inserted, negating an affirmative statement: 'they might have known' thus becomes 'they could not know', which actually makes sense in the context, where the translation is otherwise very close, so it is perhaps the mistake of a copyist.

A frequent type of misrepresentation arises where the translator chooses an ON word that has some phonetic or graphic resemblance to the OE original. Thus *to gelefenne* (49), 'to believe', having no obvious cognate in ON, is translated as *at lofa*, 'to praise' (H11); likewise the resemblance of OE *sealde* (671: past tense of *sellan*, 'to give') to ON *sáld* (H540, noun, 'measure') may have contributed to the odd translation of the whole sentence. In 158 and 678 the translator evidently recognised the verbal stem of OE *forseon*, 'to despise', and translated it as *sá*, 'saw', followed by an explanatory periphrasis. At two adjacent points (676-77 and 683-84) the OE phrase *to gebiddenne to Bel ðan gode*, 'to pray to the god Bel', is translated as *at biðia ser goðs til Bels*, 'to ask for a favour from Bel' (H545-46 and H551-52); it looks as if the translator may have confused the noun 'god' and the adjective (used as a noun) 'good' in graphic systems that did not normally distinguish vowel length at that time; but there may have been some influence from 569 and H457, where the ON *ser goðs biðia til Guðs* correctly translates the OE *bæde ... bene æt Gode*, 'to ask for a favour from God'. The influence of graphic-phonetic resemblance appears clearly in references to the devil: in the ON passage inserted after 85 (H47), where the translator (or rather perhaps a later reviser) has no OE to influence him, the devil is referred to as *fiandi*, but in all the cases where the OE text has a form of *deoful* the translation consistently has a form of *djofull* (lines 154, 291, 364, 436 and 539). Even so, there are some striking exceptions to this preference for obvious translations. For example, although OE *ælmihtig* and ON *almáttegr* occur often in the respective texts, there is no case where the latter actually translates the former: in 302, 394, 552 and 680 the OE *ælmihtig* has no counterpart in the translated text, while in 536 *þone ælmihtigan God* is translated rather laboriously as *varn Drottenn er allz er valldande*. On the other hand, ON *almáttegr* occurs in the translated text in lines H462, H520, H694 and H713, where it has no exact counterpart in the OE original, so may be the work of a reviser.

Another surprising lack of correspondence between the ON and OE texts concerns the use in Hauksbók of a probable loanword from OE. As has been pointed out by the editors of *H. edn* (p. xxx; see also *H. fac.*, *MI* 5, pp. x-xi), *Heimslýsing* in three places uses instead of the normal ON *þaðan*, 'thence', the otherwise unknown form *þanan*, presumably an adoption of OE *þanon*, 'thence'; in two of these cases (*H. edn* 152.31 and 155.34) *þanan* occurs in a text for which no OE antecedent is known (chs 3 and 4), and the third occurrence is in *De falsis diis*, line H106, where it is in a passage added independently by the translator or a copyist, which has no counterpart in Ælfric's text; but where OE *þanon* occurs in lines 426 and 544 it is not translated. It is tempting to speculate that *þanan* is a relic of the anglicised forms of ON that are believed to have circulated in England in the tenth and eleventh centuries.⁵³ If so, it is odd that it does not occur in *De falsis diis* as a translation of the corresponding OE word, but it may offer a slight piece of evidence in support of a hypothesis that other texts in this part of Hauksbók reflect an English-influenced form of Norse.

Some more complex confusion seems to be involved in the translation of the passages referring to Daniel's two spells in the lions' den (584-625 and 850-909); in both passages Ælfric follows the Vulgate closely: in the first passage there are no details of the lions and their food, but in the second the number of lions and details of their normal diet are clearly given. In the first passage, where Ælfric has *into þære leona seaðe* (588-89, 'into the lions' den') the translation has *i grof þa er dyr in oorgu lago i sjau* (MS *vij*), 'into the den that seven fierce animals lay in' (on the phrase *dyr in oorgu* in the sense 'lions' see below); here the numeral may have been inserted in anticipation of the number mentioned in line 856 (OE: not in the ON text). The account of Daniel's second spell in the lions' den presents a more complex problem. Here, as Pope noted, Ælfric lists the food given to the lions and translates the Latin *corpora*, 'bodies'(presumably meat, dead animals), with the word *leapas* (860), normally 'baskets' but here an uncommon metaphorical usage that is probably poetic (the only other recorded use in this sense is in the poem *Judith* 111). It is therefore not surprising that the translator took *leapas* in its normal sense of 'baskets' and translated it with the cognate ON word *laupa*, though this obliged him to specify some contents for what would otherwise be empty baskets. His final version, *tva laupa brauðs*, 'two baskets of bread', led the editors of Hauksbók to make

---

⁵³ Hofmann, *Nordisch-englische Lehnbeziehungen*, pp. 21-148, gives numerous examples of ON poetic texts whose language is influenced by OE; the wider implications concerning an English influenced form of Norse current in England are discussed by Roberta Frank, 'King Cnut in the verse of his skalds', p. 108. A form of Norse apparently influenced by English also occurs in the twelfth-century runic inscription in Carlisle Cathedral: see Holman, *Scandinavian Runic Inscriptions*, pp. 69-71, and Barnes and Page, *The Scandinavian Runic Inscriptions*, pp. 289-92.

the puzzled comment 'løver æder jo ikke brød' (p. CXX: 'but lions do not eat bread'); the translator was evidently unfamiliar with OE poetic usage, which may indicate that English was not his first language, but could be due to the postconquest decline of the OE poetic tradition. The change of *twa sceap*, 'two sheep', into *tiu sauði*, 'ten sheep', is a minor discrepancy, probably accidental. The number of days involved in this episode also becomes oddly changed: Ælfric, following the Vulgate closely, states that Daniel was in the lions' den for six days, and that although the lions had received their regular food until then, they were not fed while he was with them. There is a variant here in the OE text: MSS R, C and G have, with slight variations in spelling, *ac him næs þa nan geseald, þæt hi tosliton Daniel*, 'but then none was given to them so that they would devour Daniel' (Daniel 14.31, *et tunc non data sunt eis ut devorarent Danielem*), but MS L has *ac him wæs þa oftogen ælces fodan syx dagas, þæt hi þone godes mann abitan sceoldan*, 'but then all food was taken from them for six days, so that they would eat the man of God', specifying the period of time during which the lions were deprived of food (that is, the six days when Daniel was with them).[54] It is possible that the translator was working from a text like L, for this wording could be taken to imply that the lions were starved for six days before Daniel was cast into their den: only such a misunderstanding could account for the translator's paraphrase of *he þær six dagas wunode* (856-57), 'he stayed there six days', as *oc voro ljon svelt aðr sex daga til*, 'the lions were previously starved six days more', with the explanatory addition *en tolf dœgr var þeim ecki gefit til þess at þau skilldu Daniel eta oc honum grimlega bana* (H662-65), 'and for twelve days nothing was given to them so that they should devour Daniel and gruesomely kill him'. The arithmetic is impeccable but unlike that of the OE and biblical narratives, though whether the responsibility lies with the translator or a reviser is unknown.

---

[54] The variant reading in MS L here follows the wording of Ælfric's homily on St Clement: see *CH* I, p. 504 (Homily 37: Natale Sancti Clementis, lines 208-09).

One case where some corruption must be ascribed to copyists rather than to the translator is at H128-31, *en mann kyni vox þa ofund oc varð suikit af hinum sama diofli er Adam sueic fyrr*. The syntactical disjunction is obvious ('and then envy increased among mankind and [...] was betrayed by that same devil who earlier betrayed Adam') and the reference to envy (not in the OE) seems unrelated to the context; *ofund* looks like a mistake that can be corrected on the basis of the source. The OE text, *mancyn þa weox, þa wurdon hi bepæhte*, 'then mankind increased, then they were betrayed', presumably prompted a translation **Mann kynn vox . . . oc varð suikit*, and the reading in H could have arisen from miscopying an adverb supplied by the translator: a tentative emendation is *en mann kyn[n] vox þa [æfar] oc varð suikit*, 'mankind increased greatly and was betrayed'. This probably implies the assumption, plausible enough in itself, that more than one copyist was involved in successive attempts to make sense of the text, which in turn may suggest that the original translator's work was less than fully clear and idiomatic.

There may also be evidence of revision in line 280 in the description of the lecherous goddess Venus; here the OE text has *Ac hi wurðiað þa hæðenan*, 'But the heathens honour her', and the ON has *En firir henni ærðust oc heiðnir menn*, 'But heathen menn went mad for her', which is a strikingly free rendering but not quite nonsensical. Nevertheless, it is odd enough to make one wonder if the translator used the verb *ærðu*, '(they) honoured', though this would not have had a reflexive inflection, and moreover it is apparently a late loanword into ON (probably from German); conceivably it might here represent some otherwise unrecorded formation based on OE *weorðian*, but the resemblance between *wurðiað* and *ærðust* does not fully explain the translation.

These oddities in translation seldom permit a clear analysis of the processes involved. There are passages where the discrepancy between original and translation might suggest that the translation is the work of a native speaker of Norse whose understanding of the OE text was imperfect, but the discrepancy could equally represent the work of an

English translator who produced a defective or unidiomatic ON translation, which was subsequently revised by a Norse copyist to produce a text that was linguistically satisfactory but which, unknown to the reviser, did not correspond to the OE original. The Hauksbók text unfortunately gives no firm pointers to the native language of the translator, still less to his place of origin, but successive revisers were undoubtedly native speakers of a Norse language; the sentence added to the translation in H249-51, *þann er ver kollum Oðenn*, 'whom we call Odin', identifies the writer as a member of a Norse-speaking community but it is probably an explanatory comment (based on H217-18) inserted by a revisor.

Finally, one has the impression that the original translator, even if he was working in an English monastery, was somewhat isolated, perhaps the only speaker of ON in a community where the normal languages were English, French and Latin, so that his enterprise, while no doubt meeting with approval, was not subject to the criticisms of others and hence retains recurrent elements of eccentricity.

(c) Additions made in the Old Norse text

As was common in the middle ages, the translation offers not only an approximate linguistic equivalent of the original but also a certain amount of explanatory and didactic comment. Thus we are given brief notes on the fall of the angels and the creation of man after line H20, and a careful drawing of the obvious moral after line H47. The long addition after H96 seems to be prompted by the translator's omission of the negative in H93 and the need to explain the resulting mistranslation. Another passage of original comment at H139-47 includes the note on fire: *firir þvi æld at hann er varmr við at sitja*, '[they worshipped] fire because it is warm to sit beside', in contrast to the OE text that makes the point that fire is dangerous. In line 404 Ælfric, following the biblical account, lists Aaron's rod among the contents of the ark of the covenant; the translator (or a later reviser) changes this to refer to Moses' rod and then inserts an original passage on Moses and the crossing of the Red Sea (H305-

16). This change was possibly motivated by a desire to broaden the didactic scope of the homily rather than by ignorance of the biblical account or a confusion of the two rods, for immediately after this the translation expands Ælfric's reference to the tables of the law (406-09) and adds, quite correctly, that the contents of the ark included manna from the exile in the wilderness (H317-28: in 403-04 Ælfric had mentioned *se heofonlica mete*, 'the heavenly food'), but the translation introduces the biblical word 'manna' (H324) followed by an explanation. This addition was clearly made by someone who was prepared to consult the Bible in order to amplify the homily, and since, as has already been pointed out, there are passages where the translation makes mistakes that could have been corrected by reference to the biblical source, one may deduce that the original translator, while not necessarily an unlearned man, found the task of translating so demanding that he did not attempt to set his work in a wider intellectual or religious context; additions such as the reference to manna may then be presumed to be the work of a well informed and thoughtful reviser, who could conceivably have been the translator when subsequently relieved of whatever pressure the task of translation imposed, but is more likely to have been a later copyist, whether or not the Hauksbók scribe.

One addition, clearly by one or more later copyists, is of interest for the light it casts on the world in which the translation cirulated: in lines 447-50 Ælfric paraphrases the biblical account of the plagues that afflicted the Philistines (Vulgate I Regum 5.6): *Heom comon to eac mys manega geond þæt land and heora æceras aweston and ðone eard fordydon*, 'there also came to them many mice throughout that country and laid waste their fields and destroyed the land'. The Norse text as originally transcribed in Hauksbók reads *Mys oc maðkar a lande þvi ato korn alt firir monnum, oc firirforo landenu ollu*, 'mice and maggots in that land devoured all the people's corn and destroyed all the land', and one notes here the addition of unbiblical 'maggots', perhaps because mice were not thought of as seriously destructive pests whereas some kind of maggots were a more familiar danger to crops. This adaptation for a local audience is augmented by two further insertions in Hauksbók: after *maðkar* the words *ok lemendr*, 'and lemmings', are inserted above the line, introducing a more typically Norwegian animal, which can damage roots by its burrowing, and in the right-hand margin is added *oc gras retr oc viðar retr*, 'and grass-roots and tree-roots', further specifying the crops liable to damage by pests (the insertions are very unclear because of the use of a chemical reagent, both are probably in the same hand, not that of the main scribe).[55] The addition was apparently made after the text had been written in Hauksbók in order to make the biblical story clearer to a Norwegian or Icelandic audience.

Reference has already been made to peculiarities in the translation of Ælfric's account of Daniel's second spell in the lions' den; the same episode is even more striking for an addition to the original text which has the effect of transforming the biblical world of the story. The Babylonians, offended by the destruction of their dragon, make their complaint in terms that have no counterpart in Ælfric or the Bible but draw instead on Old Norse law for the sentence *letust ubotabol hafa fengit af Daniel*, 'they say that they have suffered from Daniel an offence for which no compensation could be accepted' (H644-45). The principle of compensation for offences suffered or comitted is of course fundamental to Norse law, and the *óbótaböl*, an offence so serious that no compensation can be accepted for it, figures prominently in Icelandic sagas, but the appearance of such a term in this context is surprising. Moreover, it is matched by what follows: *oc gengu aller til konungs oc buðu honum koste tva: at hann seldi þeim i hendr Daniel, elligar skylldi þeir drepa hann*

---

[55] Taylor, p. 104, makes the interesting point that in MS AM 764 4° *lemendr* translates *locustae*, citing Kaalund, *ANF* 25 (1909), 302; see however *Kulturhistorisk Leksikon*, s.v. *Lämlar*, where it is pointed out that lemmings continue to be referred to as destructive creatures by Icelandic writers who were probably no longer aware of the exact nature of these animals. Taylor's further suggestion that the reference to the destruction of roots implies volcanic activity, and hence an Icelandic origin for this insertion, is less plausible.

sialfan oc alla hans ætt, 'they all went to the king and offered him two choices: that he should give Daniel into their hands or else they would kill him and all his family' (H646-51). The offer of two choices, death or compliance, is a prominent saga motif,[56] so that in these sentences the world of the Old Testament is transmuted into the medieval world of Icelandic sagas. It is particularly striking in this context that the phrase *drepa hann sialfan oc alla hans ætt*, 'kill [the king] himself and all his family', does not quite correspond to Ælfric's phraseology (*elles we þe ofsleað*, 'otherwise we will kill you') but expands it on the basis of the Bible (Vulgate, Daniel 14.28, *interficiemus te et domum tuum*). The phrase *sakar þessa nauðarkostz*, 'as a result of this threat' (H652-53), is likewise not in Ælfric but also shows biblical influence (Daniel 14.29, *necessitate compulsus*), and the whole sequence of events in this portion of the translation is closer to the Bible than to Ælfric. The translation of lines H643-58 thus treats the OE text with unaccustomed freedom in two ways: first, it makes use of the Bible to interpret and rewrite Ælfric, and secondly, it uses phraseology and motifs that reflect a knowledge of an established ON literary style, the legal term *óbótaböl* and the saga-motif of *tveir kostir*. The first of these features is remarkable because it is untypical of this text; the second has a parallel in H471-72, *konungren varðe þat mal*: here too the translation introduces a legal phrase, *verja mál*, 'to defend a lawsuit' (here perhaps rather 'rejected the accusation'), but the rest of the sentence, *oc qvast þat eigi vilia*, 'and said that he would not' (H472), is an independent addition with all the easy directness of saga-dialogue. In this episode Ælfric follows the Bible in being primarily interested in the king's struggle with his conscience, but the translation emphasises instead the king's struggle with his nobles, reflecting the interests of so many of the family sagas and kings' sagas.

---

[56] For example, *Njáls saga*, ch. 76; *Hrafnkels saga Freysgoða*, chs 13 and 16; and *Gísla saga*, chs 1 and 3; see *Njáls saga*, ed. Sveinsson; *Hrafnkels Saga Freysgoða*, ed. Helgason, pp. 25.10 and 37.7; *Gísla Saga Súrssonar*, ed. Loth, pp. 1.15 and 5.1-2.

The conclusion to be drawn from the unusual features in these passages seems fairly obvious: the ON text as it has come down to us in Hauksbók is the result of at least two stages of work: first, an original translation that does not fully or clearly represent Ælfric's OE, does not consult the Bible where it might have helped, and does not reflect mastery of an established Norse literary tradition; and second, a revision of isolated passages (at least H471-75 and H643-54, and perhaps more) by one or more revisers capable of modifying the text in the light of the Vulgate Bible and conforming to an established tradition of ON literary style.

The work of one or more revisers also appears in one further piece of lexical evidence. At most points where the OE text has the word *leon*, 'lion', the translation uses the word *dýr*, 'animal', either alone (H498, H511), or in a periphrasis, *dyr in óörgu* (H470, H477, H656) or *dyr in ólmu* (H492-93, H523-24), both meaning 'the fierce animals', which may have been prompted by the OE *wið ða rædan deor*, 'against the fierce animals' (653); 'lion' is omitted altogether at line 883-84, H686, where *to ðære leona seaðe* is rendered *til grafar þeirar*. In H658, however, is (as mentioned above) an inserted sentence with no counterpart in Ælfric, *oc voro lion svelt aðr sex daga til*, using the ON *ljón* instead of *dýr*; in 859, H660, *leonum* is translated *dyrlionen*, in 874, H676 the OE *on þam pytte* is rendered *til lionagrafar þeirar*, and in 912, H720 *of þære deora seaðe* becomes *or þeiri liona grof*. The use of the word *ljón* is thus restricted to the final part of the Norse version of the Daniel story (lines 850-917) and first appears in the portion where there is reason to believe, on the evidence of some independent use of the Bible and the appearance of ON legal terminology, that the text includes the work of a reviser. From this one might infer that the original translator did not know, or for some stylistic reason preferred to avoid, an ON derivative of the Latin *leo*. Even so, the fact remains that the periphrasis *dyr in óörgu* has a long history of literary usage, particularly but not exclusively with reference to lions, and one cannot know how well this usage was established at the time when the phrase was used in the ON *De falsis diis*.[57] The inference is that the ON text was copied, with various changes, on more than one occasion before it underwent the final revision and abridgement on being copied into Hauksbók. The passage on the Six Ages of the World (lines H742-61), expanding Ælfric's brief reference in line 930, is essentially an independent conclusion that was probably written to round off the work when it was decided to omit the last part of the original homily, presumably by the scribe who copied the text into Hauksbók, and, unlike earlier parts of the homily described in more detail below, it shows the stylistic fluency of an experienced writer.

The separate stages of revision and their exact extent are of course uncertain, but the most obvious signs of rewriting are concentrated in the last part of the extant text, and, considering the time lapse between the initial translation and the final copying into Hauksbók, it is probably surprising that so much of Ælfric's homily is still so clearly recognisable in the extant ON text. It has been argued above that the original translation was probably made in England, but whatever revisions took place are much more likely to have been made during the copying processes that continued after the text was taken to Norway or Iceland. Whatever copying occurred must also have involved at some stage, perhaps indeed repeatedly, the making of whatever adjustments were necessary to modernise the language, so that, as already said, analysis of the language reveals nothing of the date or place of the original translation or of the native language of the translator.

(d) Some stylistic features of the translation

When this text is compared with other early ON homilies and saints' lives, a noticeable feature of the translation is its relatively restricted vocabulary. When certain phrases in the ON text are compared with the OE original it becomes clear

---

[57] See Beck, '*Hit óarga dýr*'; I am indebted to Professor Beck for a copy of this article.

that Ælfric could command a wider lexical variety than the translator. For example, in lines 153-55, where Ælfric uses the two verbs *bepæhte* and *beswac* ('deceived and betrayed'), the translation has only one (*svikit* and *sveic* respectively); likewise, in lines 246-52 the OE sequence *saca – wrohte – wawan – gefeoht* ('conflict, contention, trouble, fighting') is translated by *hernaðe – orostu – orostu*. In some cases the translation uses words that were probably more colloquial than the corresponding, perhaps more literary, words in the original, while some English words are simply omitted: compare for example lines 73-74, *on yðum urne færlice*, 'ran suddenly over the waves', with *gengi a se*, 'walked on the sea'; or *swyðlic and wælhreow*, 'mighty and cruel' (205-06) with *illr maðr*; or *hetol and pwyrlic*, 'malignant and perverse' (214-15) with *illr oc grimr*; or *mærostan*, 'most glorious' (231) with *bestum*; or *stala and leasbrednysse*, 'stealing and deceit' (263), with *stela oc liuga*, 'to steal and lie'; or *gif ge þonne æteowiað*, 'if you then demonstrate' (717), with *ef þer segit mer þat satt*, 'if you tell me it is true'. At times this relative paucity of vocabulary, suggestive of colloquial rather than literary style, seems matched by a certain awkwardness of syntax or a tendency to wordiness: compare for example in lines 410-12, where *ða hæðenan* is translated *þeir hinu heiðnu menn*, and *mid þam heofenlican haligdome* becomes *með þeim miclum helgum dome er or hifnum kom*. One cannot avoid the impression that the original translator had limited skills in writing the Norse language, which need not necessarily indicate that a form of Norse was not his native language, but may suggest that he was working at a date when an ON literary style was not yet fully developed.

Finally, one might note that there is an approximate stylistic resemblance between Ælfric's rhythmic alliterative prose and some ON religious prose of later date than this translation, both showing a consciously shaped style characterised by rhythmic and alliterative patterning, but there is none of this kind of stylistic manipulation in the translation of *De falsis diis*.[58] Where alliterative phrases occur they are of a traditional colloquial or proverbial kind, like *rikir oc ramir* (H154), *i morðe oc i manndrape* (H205-06), *or steinum . . . or stocum* (H261-62), *suma við minna en suma við meira* (H279-80). There are occasional passages that could perhaps be interpreted as an uneasy imitation of verse-like patterning:

> fyst þa stund er þau gettu   boðorða Guðs
> þa matte þeim ecki   at angre verða   (H30-33)

> þa fundu þeir guð sitt   a golfe liggia
> firir orkenni niðri   sem hann beði friðar   (H339-41).

But the resemblance may be coincidental, for the prose in general does not look like the work of a conscious stylist.

---

[58] See Tveitane, *Den lærde Stil*. Abram, 'Scandinavian context', pp. 440-42, finds English-influenced phrasal patterning in some original Norse homilies.

OTHER TEXTS IN HAUKSBÓK CONNECTED WITH ÆLFRIC'S WORKS

As explained above, *De falsis diis* commonly occurs in manuscripts together with a group of other works by Ælfric, the *Sermo in laetania maiore* (also known as *De auguriis*) and the OE translations of *Interrogationes Sigewulfi* and *De duodecim abusivis*. The connection between *De auguriis* and *Heimslýsing* ch. 9 has long been recognised,[59] and there is also a possible connection between Ælfric's *De duodecim abusivis* and another passage in Hauksbók (*H. edn* p. 185, 21-27).[60] The relationship between the OE and ON texts of *De duodecim abusivis* is not clear, but the latter is apparently not entirely independent of the former. The Latin text opens with a list of common faults in the first paragraph (*sapiens sine operibus, senex sine religione*: 'a wise man without good works, an old man without religion', and so on), and then continues in paragraph 2 as follows:

> Haec sunt duodecim abusiva saeculi per quae saeculi rota, si in illo fuerint, decipitur et ad tartari tenebras nullo impediente iustitiae suffragio per iustum Dei iudicium rotatur.[61]

> These are the twelve abuses of the age, through which, if they should be present in it, the whole age is deceived and turned to the darkness of hell, unless the intervention of justice by a just God puts a stop to it.

The OE version retains the Latin text of the list of common faults and continues in English with the translation of the second paragraph:

> Twelf unþeawas syndon on þissere worulde to hearme eallum mannum gif hi moton ricsian, and he alecgað rihtwisnysse and

---

[59] Reichborn-Kjennerud, 'Et Kapitel i Hauksbók', 144-48.
[60] Noted by J. Turville-Petre, 'Sources', p. 176, n.2; for previous discussion of the ON texts of *De duodecim abusivis* see Seip, *Nye Studier*, p. 60, and *H. fac.*, p. xix, n.23.
[61] *Pseudo-Cyprianus de XII Abusivis Saeculi*, ed. Hellmann, p. 32. None of the Latin versions described by Hellmann changes the order of the opening paragraphs.

þone geleafan amyrrað, and mancynn gebringað gif hi moton to helle.⁶²

There are twelve abuses in this world, harmful to all men if they are allowed to flourish, and they suppress righteousness and destroy the faith, and, if they can, bring mankind to hell.'

This is then followed by the translation of the list of faults as set out in the first paragraph of the Latin text (*se wita butan godum weorcum*, and so on), so that the English text effectively reverses the order of the first two paragraphs.

The short ON text in Hauksbók retains the arrangement of the OE text, placing the second paragraph of the Latin text first and following it with the list of abuses, though in other respects the text in Hauksbók is closer to the Latin than to the OE, as in the concluding reference to justice:

Þesser eru xij heims osomar þeir er tela allt veralldar lif þar er þeir verða framdir, ok draga þa til helvitiss er þeim fylgia, sva at eingi rettletis vorn hlifir þeim.⁶³

These are the twelve evils of the world, which ensnare all worldly life where they are encouraged, and bring those who follow them to the punishments of hell, as long as no just defence restrains them.

It is possible that the ON text was written by someone who had before him both the Latin and OE texts, but more probable that a text based on the OE was later revised by referring to the Latin text. In the list of abuses the ON text is closer to the Latin than to the OE, especially in following the Latin distinction between *plebs* and *populus* (*þioð* and *lyðr*) where the OE translates both as *folc*; the order of the first two paragraphs is the only respect in which the Hauksbók text appears to follow the English version.

There does not seem to be any direct connection between Ælfric's translation of Alcuin's *Interrogationes Sigewulfi* and any text in Hauksbók, though there is an obvious community of interest at certain points. *Heimslýsing* ch. 15,

---

[62] Quoted from *Old English Homilies*, p. 299; other versions of the English text in print (see n. 9 above) are substantially the same.
[63] Quoted from *H. edn*, p. 185. 21-23: *Heimspeki ok helgifræði*, ch. 5.

Vm regnboga (*H. edn* pp. 174. 30 to 175. 11), is on the same subject, the allegorical interpretation of the colours of the rainbow, as *Interrogationes* no. 135 (Ælfric's translation lines 360-67), but where Alcuin's Latin text, followed by Ælfric, offers comment on only two colours, red and blue, the ON text adds a third, yellow.[64] *Heimslýsing* ch. 7 (*H. edn* pp. 164. 35 to 165. 25), on the settlement of the earth by Noah's sons, is on the same theme as *Interrogationes* nos. 141-42 (Ælfric's translation lines 367-78), but here again Hauksbók shows a somewhat different treatment of the theme and cannot have been translated from either Alcuin's Latin or Ælfric's OE. A continuous passage of Ælfric's *Interrogationes*, lines 360-83, has a number of parallels in Hauksbók, beginning with the two pieces just mentioned and concluding with a portion of *Heimslýsing* ch. 3, on the building of Babylon (*H. edn* p. 153. 29-33: compare *De falsis diis* lines P73-76), but these parallels are probably due to the independent use of similar material, not to translation. Such summaries of biblical material and basic religious doctrine were common in the middle ages, and the ON compiler may have used a range of sources from Isidore of Seville to Honorius of Autun.[65]

The OE version of *De duodecim abusivis* had only a very minor effect on Hauksbók, and Ælfric's *Interrogationes Sigewulfi* had no direct effect at all; on the other hand, *De falsis diis* is translated at length and in considerable detail. In between these comes Ælfric's *De auguriis*, which accounts for several details in *Heimslýsing* ch. 9, though the latter is not a full translation or even a continuous paraphrase of the OE text.

---

[64] The Latin and OE texts are printed in 'Ælfric's version', ed. MacLean, pp. 38-39; another interpretation, differing from both *Interrogationes* and Hauksbók, is offered by Bede in his *Commentary on Genesis*: see *PL* 91, col. 227.

[65] For details see Þorkelsson, *Nökkur Blöð*.

THE OLD ENGLISH AND OLD NORSE TEXTS OF *DE AUGURIIS*

(a) Introductory

Ælfric's *Sermo in laetania maiore*, commonly called *De auguriis* because it is partly based on a Latin homily of that title, is included among the Lives of Saints in MS W, and was printed as *LS* XVII by Skeat.[66] There are various problems concerning the sources of Ælfric's *De auguriis* and *Heimslýsing* ch. 9 that need not be tackled here: the present concern is to compare the English and Norse texts and to establish in what respects the latter is derived from the former.

Ælfric's *De auguriis* is a somewhat discursive work, having the weakness, common to many medieval sermons, of aiming at several different targets. As is normal with Ælfric, the homily is an amalgamation of a variety of sources; only the central portion (lines 65-207) is indebted to the pseudo-Augustinian homily referred to in line 67, and even within this portion there is much that is not from that source. The Latin homily, *De auguriis*, is not in fact by Augustine, though it was commonly ascribed to him in Anglo-Saxon times.[67] It is now accepted that it is by Caesarius Arlatensis.[68] Ælfric's homily begins (lines 1-46) in prose with an exposition of St Paul's teaching on the theme of Christian morality, including (lines 34-37) a quotation from 1 Corinthians 6. 9-10. Cont-

---

[66] Skeat prints the rubric *Sermo sancto* (sic) *Augustini de auguriis* from MS C (MS D in Skeat's sigla: Cambridge, Corpus Christi College, MS 303): on the illegible heading in Hauksbók, which apparently referred to Augustine, see above p. 21.

[67] For example, by St Boniface, who quotes from the homily in a letter: see *Die Briefe des heiligen Bonifatius und Lullius*, ed. Tangl, I. 85, Epistola 50.

[68] As a pseudo-Augustinian work the homily is printed in *PL* 39, cols 2268-71, Sermo 'De auguriis'; this was first recognised as Ælfric's source by Förster, 'Altenglische Predigtquellen: 2. Pseudo-Augustin und Ælfric'. As an authentic work by Caesarius it is printed in *Caesarii Arlatensis sermones*, ed. Morin. The text is substantially the same in both editions; in the following discussion I refer to Morin's edition. See further Traherne, 'Caesarius of Arles'.

inuing in his characteristic rhythmic prose (line 47 onwards) Ælfric selects from St Paul's list of transgressions the sin of idolatry but interprets it in a general sense as devotion to ungodly practices (lines 47-66). At this point Ælfric claims to begin quoting Augustine: *Augustinus se snotera bisceop sæde on sumere boc* (line 67: 'Augustine, the wise bishop, said in a certain book'); there follows a denunciation of various kinds of superstition and paganism (lines 67-165), leading to a statement of the limitations of the power of the devil over the Christian (lines 166-207); the final section of the homily (lines 208-71) is a disquisition on foreknowledge, predestination, free will and moral responsibility. It may be appropriate to apply the title, *Sermo in laetania maiore* (used in three manuscripts), to the whole homily and to restrict the title *De auguriis* (used in four manuscripts) to the central portion on pagan superstitions (lines 65-207), which is based on the Latin homily of that name by Caesarius; since it is this portion that is drawn on in Hauksbók the shorter title will be used here.

Ælfric's use of this source follows his usual practice (as in, for example, his use of Martin of Braga in *De falsis diis*): he translates or paraphrases some passages, omits others, occasionally reorders portions and adds original passages or extracts from other sources. Lines 68-83 and 166-207 of Ælfric's *De auguriis* derive from a sequence of extracts from the Latin homily; there is no continuous translation but numerous lines are translated from lines extracted from the Latin source. In all, nearly forty lines of Ælfric's text have close parallels in Caesarius, but Ælfric also adds details from other sources. There are three main additions that are not in Caesarius. First, lines 84-87: the casting of lots may be permissible for some purposes but not for divination. Second, 100-65: auguries are a form of sorcery and witches are guided by devils; magicians brought about Pharaoh's downfall, but Simon the sorcerer was overcome by Peter; do not consult witches about your health and do not take offerings to stones, trees and springs; the Christian must protect himself against the devil by making the sign of the cross; some women go to crossroads and draw their children through the earth, leading to their own and their children's damnation; other women kill unborn children, damning them as well as themselves; others make love-potions; the Christian must avoid all such. And third, 177-89: God sometimes allows the devil to afflict us but He will care for us. For this additional material Ælfric used a variety of sources, mainly well known writings on superstition. For example, the passage on pagan offerings at stones, trees and springs (129-31) was clearly suggested by the main source (Caesarius's condemnation of offerings at trees and springs) but the reference to stones is added from some other source, probably Eligius.[69] In their lists of places where pagan rites are practised Martin of Braga, Eligius and Pirminius all mention crossroads;[70] for Martin crossroads are sacred to Mercury (*De correctione rusticorum*, ch. 7, translated by Ælfric in *De falsis diis*, lines 264-67) and are also the location of rites involving the lighting of candles (Martin, ch. 16, not translated by Ælfric); crossroads are associated with candles and votive offerings by Eligius, and with wooden images and dancing by Pirminius in the passages just cited. One or more of these passages probably suggested Ælfric's reference to rites at crossroads in *De auguriis* 148-49: *Eac sume gewitlease wif farað to wega gelætum / and teoð heora cild þurh ða eorðan*, 'some foolish women go to crossroads and draw their child through the earth'. The nature of the ritual has however been changed by Ælfric, perhaps because he was not familiar with rites involving candles and other offerings at crossroads, but was familiar with a superstitious ritual (or at any rate with the condemnation of such a ritual) involving children; further light is cast on this passage by the Norse translation in Hauksbók and this subject is explored more fully below. Ælfric's ensuing condemnation of abortions and the killing of illegitimate children (*De auguriis*, lines 151-56) is not in

[69] Audoenus of Rouen, *Vita Eligii*, II. 16: *MGH*, Script. rer. Merov., IV. 705: 'ad petras aut ad fontes vel ad arbores'.
[70] Martin and Eligius as cited; Pirminius, *Scarapsus*, ed. Jecker, ch. 22 (p. 54).

his main pseudo-Augustinian source, but it is a recurrent theme in patristic writings, appearing in (among other places) other homilies by Caesarius and also in Pirminius.[71]

The central portion of Ælfric's homily (lines 100-65), which is not based on the Latin *De auguriis*, is important because the Norse translation in Hauksbók draws on it, thus showing, as was pointed out by Reichborn-Kjennerud, that the writer did not draw independently on Ælfric's Latin sources. The same argument applies here as was advanced by Pope concerning the ON translation of *De falsis diis*. In the case of *De falsis diis* the fact that the Norse version is translated from the OE is quite clear and is confirmed by frequent close verbal resemblances and occasional striking misunderstandings like *laupa brauðs* for *leapas*. The case of *De auguriis* is rather less obvious because, in the first place, the Norse text (probably as revised rather than as originally translated) treats Ælfric much as Ælfric had treated Caesarius: it omits passages, rearranges portions and adds substantial passages from other sources; and secondly, there is a lack of conclusive verbal resemblances, not to mention peculiarities like *leapas-laupa*. The text of *De auguriis* in Hauksbók has been subjected to a more complex process of revision and rewriting than is the case with *De falsis diis*.

Nevertheless, the Norse writer's debt to Ælfric is clear in many basic correspondences between the two texts, the most important of which are set out below. Quotations are from the published editions, but since Skeat only used four of the eight extant manuscripts of *De auguriis*, a survey of textual variants (not attempted here) might reveal further correspondences with the ON text.

---

[71] *Caesarii Arlatensis sermones*, Sermon no. 1, pp. 8-9; no. 20, pp. 90-91; no. 51.4, p. 229; no. 52.4, p. 231; and no. 200, pp. 809-10. Pirminius, *Scarapsus*, ch. 21, p. 54.

(b) Comparative table of the Old English and Old Norse texts of *De auguriis*

De auguriis	*Hauksbók*
Augustinus se snotera bisceop sæde eac on sumere bec, Mine gebroðra þa leofstan, gelome ic eow warnode and mid fæderlicre carfulnysse ic eow cuðlice manode þæt ge andsætan wiglunge þe unwise men healdað (67-70)	Hin helgi byskup er heitir Agustinus melti við þa menn er hann var kenni-maðr yfir, Goðer bræðr, quað hann, oft vara ec yðr oc kenni ec yðr sua sem faðer skal kenna bornum sinum, at þer fylgit eigi golldrum nema gerningum illum (167, 12-15)
Ne sceal nan man cepan be dagum on hwilcum dæge he fare oððe on hwylcum he gecyrre, forðan þe god gesceop ealle ða seofan dagas þe yrnað on þære wucan oð þysre worulde geendunge; ac se ðe hwider faran wille, singe his paternoster and credan gif he cunne and clypige to his dryhten, and bletsige hine sylfne, and siðige orsorh þurh godes gescyldnysse butan ðæra sceoccena wiglunga (92-99)	Menn skolu ecki dagraðs leita at syslu sinni eða for sina a þeim degi er honum lizt ser haglegastr oc veðr er gott oc mela sua at ec byria verc mitt eða for nima i nafne alamttegs guðs; hann se hialp min oc fulting a þessum degi oc sua a huerium annara er yfir kemr, ver skolum var væl geta með diofuls suicum oc sua oss vandlega signa með guðs pinslar marke, en þat er cross drottens vars; ver skolum gera hann a oss með retri tru oc lata oss þann cross i hug koma er drottenn var pindr a, þa er fiandenn reddare við hann (168, 36-169, 8)
We sceolan on ælcne timan and on ælcre styrunge gebletsian us sylfe mid soðum geleafan and mid rod tacne þa reðan aflian (143-45)	
Ne sceal se cristena befrinan þa fulan wiccan be his gesundfulnysse (124-45)	Eigi skolu cristnir menn spyria galdra menn nema gerninga at heilendis fare sinu (167, 21-22)

Eac sume gewitlease wif farað to wega gelætum and teoð heora cild þurh ða eorðan, and swa deofle betæcað hi sylfe and heora bearn (148-50)

En þær ero sumar er taka born sin oc ganga til gatna motz oc draga þau þar i giognum iorð ... oc vitu þer eigi þa huessu mioc er þer festa þa born sin oc sialfar sic a hendi dioflenum (167, 32-36)

Nu ero þeir sumir menn er sua obeint sea sitt mal at þeir drygia hordom saman fyst oc gera born saman, en siðan þa tuefallda þau sua sinn glæp at þau kosta þess at firirfara barnenu fyr en fætt verði, firir þui at menn skolu eigi vita glæp þeira oc ero þau reddare við mennena en við guð; en þeira misgerninga ero ogorlega oc endalaust morð; þa firirferst barnet heiðit oc sua hinn illi faðer oc sua hin illa moðer, nema þau gange til skrifta oc iðrist æ meðan þau lifa. (168, 11-18)

Sume hi acwellað heora cild ærðam þe hi acennede beon oððe æfter acennednysse, þæt hi cuðe ne beon ne heora mannfulla forligr ameldod ne wurðe, ac heora yfel is egeslic and endeleaslic morð; þær losað þæt cild laðlice hæðen and seo arlease modor butan heo hit æfre gebete. (151-56)

Sume hi wyrcað heora wogerum drencas oððe sumne wawan þæt hi hi to wife habbon. (157-78)

En þer ero sumar konor er gera drycki oc gefa gilmonnum sinum til þess at þæir skili þa unna þeim vel oc hafa þer at konum ser. (168, 18-21)

Ac þyllice sceandas sceolan siðian to helle þær hi æfre cwylmiað on þam cwealmbærum fyre and on egeslicum witum for heora gewitleaste. (159-61)

En þer arg holur er með slicu fara vita seti sitt æ i brennanda ældi oc i endalausum quolum nema þer gange til skrifta oc bæti glæp sinn. (168, 21-23)

(c) Aspects of the Old Norse *De auguriis*

While *H. edn* 169, lines 4-8, was apparently suggested by *De Auguriis*, lines 144-47, it may also owe something to Ælfric's homily 'Exaltatio Sancte Crucis' (*LS* XXVII), lines 153-54; a copy of this homily is preserved in MS L immediately after *De falsis diis* and *De auguriis*. The relevant passages are as follows:-

> *H. edn* 169, 4-8: Ver skolum var væl geta með djofuls svicum oc sva oss vandlega signa með guðs pinslar marke, en þat er cross drottens vars; ver skolum gera hann a oss með retri tru, oc lata oss þann cross þa i hug koma er drottenn var var pindr a; þa er fjandenn reddare við hann helldr en við ecki vapn.

> We should guard against the devil's treachery and carefully sign ourselves with the token of God's passion, that is our Lord's cross; we should do that to ourselves with true faith, and call to mind the cross that our Lord suffered on; then the devil will be more frightened of that than by any weapon.

> *LS* XVII, 143-47: We sceolan on ælcne timan and on ælcere styrunge gebletsian us sylfe mid soðum geleafan, and mid rode-tacne þa reðan aflian; for ðan þe se reða deofol wearð þurh ða rode oferswiðed, and heo is ure sige-beacn ongean þone sceoccan a.

> We should on every occasion and in every trouble cross ourselves with true faith, and by the sign of the cross put to flight the wicked ones; because the wicked devil was overcome by the cross, and it is always our sign of victory against the devil.

> *LS* XXVII, 153-54: and se reða feond bið sona afyrht for ðam sigefæstan tacne.

> and the wicked fiend will immediately be frightened by the victorious sign.

The context of this last sentence is also on the theme of overcoming the devil with the sign of the cross.

The theme common to *LS* XXVII and the Hauksbók homily, but missing from *LS* XVII, is the devil's fear of the cross (*se reða feond bið sona afyrht*: *þa er fjandenn reddare*), and the verbal correspondence between *fjandenn* and *feond* (where the relevant phrase in *LS* XVII has *deofol*) supports this parallel; but the ON writer could perhaps have arrived at this phrase by working independently from a Latin source.

The following passages in Hauksbók are not based on *LS* XVII: *H. edn* 167, 17-21, 30-32; 167, 37-168, 11; and 169, 8-39; none of these passages has any parallel in the homily by Caesarius that was Ælfric's main source. Like Ælfric's homilies, the ON text combines materials from a variety of sources, especially in the final portion of the homily. The other sources are likely to have been Latin and a number of parallels may be noted:-

> *H. edn* 169, 14-15: Augustine, *PL* 40, cols 1192-3, lines 68-69, and Alcuin's adaptation of this passage in *PL* 101, col. 1208, lines 19-20.
>
> *H. edn* 169, 15-19: *PL* 40, col. 1193, lines 3-6, and *PL* 101, col. 1208, lines 32-35.
>
> *H. edn* 169, 21-30: *PL* 40, col. 1192, line 3, and perhaps *PL* 101, col. 1208, lines 20-29 (where Alcuin omits the second part of Augustine's interpretation); but the Norse author may also have used the more detailed interpretation developed by Bede (*PL* 92, cols 615-16) or Haymo (*PL* 118, col. 440).[72]
>
> *H. edn* 169, 30-31: perhaps suggested by Alcuin (*PL* 101, col. 1208, lines 29-31): these lines are not in Augustine (*PL* 40, cols 1192-93), so this piece of evidence conflicts with that of *H. edn* 169, 21-30, which points to the use of Augustine's original version rather than Alcuin's recension of it; the ON writer may have worked from a conflated text different from those printed by Migne in *Patrologia Latina*. The allegorisation of the cross also appears in OHG in Otfrid's *Evangelienbuch* V.1.[73]

---

[72] Both Bede and Haymo follow Augustine in deriving this interpretation from Ephesians 3.18, and they follow the biblical order in their list: (i) *latitudo*, indicating the crosspiece of the cross, (ii) *longitudo*, the upright below the crosspiece, (iii) *altitudo*, the upright above the crosspiece, (iv) *profunditas*, the part of the cross buried in the ground. The text in H changes this order, taking the parts of the cross in the order iii –i – ii – iv. The whole of *H. edn* 169, 15-30, is paralleled in *Gamal norsk Homiliebok*, ed. Indrebø, pp. 103-04 (see also p. 80, 23-27), and *Homiliubók*, ed. Wisén, p. 38; this homily cites Sedulius as a source, presumably *Carmen Paschale* 185-92 (see *PL* 19, col. 724).

[73] See Otfrid, *Evangelienbuch*, ed. Erdmann, pp. 218-19: reference from Kaske, 'A poem of the cross'.

Heimslýsing, ch. 9, as it stands may be the work of more than one writer: it is an eclectic compilation from a range of sources, but what is important in the present connection is that one of the sources used was a now lost ON translation, perhaps even a close and complete translation, of Ælfric's *De auguriis*, and fragments of this are preserved in Hauksbók. The alternative, that the extracts from Ælfric were translated piecemeal for the ON text, is less credible.

In spite of the opening reference to Augustine in the homily in Hauksbók, it is not likely that the writer knew the pseudo-Augustinian homily for he includes nothing from it that is not in Ælfric's OE version, and the reference to Augustine is taken from Ælfric; as Reichborn-Kjennerud pointed out, the ON text is always closer to the OE than to the Latin original in the parallel passages. The ON treatment of the OE text is however highly selective: in all, fewer than thirty lines (as printed by Skeat) are translated, the extracts ranging from single lines to sequences of half a dozen lines. The compiler's concern was not simply to reproduce one source, or even to give a fairly loose rendering of the kind found in parts of the ON *De falsis diis*, but to produce a new work, based on various sources, Latin and OE (presumably in ON translation), and retaining reference only to those abuses and practices that he judged relevant to his envisaged audience.

Among the passages reproduced from the OE is one that is transformed from the pseudo-Augustinian source, the denunciation of pagan rites at crossroads (*LS* XVII, 148-56), which deserves further discussion because of its intrinsic interest and the light it throws on a range of Anglo-Scandinavian connections. As pointed out above, where Martin of Braga condemns a candle-lighting ritual at crossroads, Ælfric refers to a rite apparently not mentioned in any classical or patristic source. The details and purpose of the rite are not explained but it involved taking a child and 'drawing it through the earth' at crossroads. The inference is that Ælfric here records a practice that had some currency in Anglo-Saxon England: the rite is mentioned in several

Anglo-Saxon sources, both Latin and vernacular, but is apparently uncommon in continental records; in particular, it is mentioned in the OE version of the *Poenitentiale Pseudo-Ecgberti*, but not in its Frankish Latin source, the Penitential of Halitgar.[74] Ælfric's reference is as follows:

> Eac sume gewitlease wif farað to wega gelætum
> and teoð heora cild þurh ða eorðan,
> and swa deofle betæcað hi sylfe and heora bearn. (*LS* XVII, 148-50)

> Þær losað þæt cild laðlice hæðen
> and seo arleasa modor, butan heo hit æfre gebete. (*LS* XVII, 155-56)

> And some stupid women also go to crossroads and draw their child through the earth, and so consign themselves and their children to the devil ... thus that child is lost as a loathsome heathen, and its disgraceful mother too, unless she should ever make atonement for it.

Corresponding to this *Heimslýsing*, ch. 9 (*H. edn* 167, 32-37) has:

> En þær ero sumar er taka born sin oc ganga til gatna-motz oc draga þau þar i gjognum jorð til heilsu þeim, oc til þess at þau

---

[74] The fullest list of references to this rite is collected in Kittredge, *Witchcraft*, pp. 31 and 386 (n. 66); see also Jente, *Die mythologischen Ausdrücke*, pp. 57-58 and 306-07. For Anglo-Latin references see *Poenitentiale Theodori*, ed. Thorpe, XXVII.16, p. 83: 'Si quis pro sanitate filioli per foramen terrae exierit ...'; and *Poenitentiale Pseudo-Ecgberti*, ed. Raith, p. 55: 'Qui puerum ... per foramen defossae terrae duxerit ...' For OE references see *Poenitentiale Pseudo-Ecgberti* IV.16, p. 55: 'Wifman ... gif heo tilað hire cild mid ænigum wiccecræfte oððe æt wega gelætan þurh þa eorðan tyhð'; *Wulfstan's Canons of Edgar*, ed. Fowler, no 16 (MS Junius), p. 5: 'ðone deofles cræft þær man þa cild þurh þa eorðan tihð'. Anonymous homily, ed. Assmann, p. 149: 'And þæt nan man ne sece to nanre wellan, ne to nanum stane, ne to nanum treowe, ne nan man his cild þurh þa eorðan ne teo, forðam se ðe þæt deð, he betæcð þæt cild eallum deoflum and seo moder forð mid'. The only continental reference I know is in the 'Corrector' of Burchard of Worms, *Decretum*, Lib. XIX: see *PL* 140, col. 974 D, and *Die Bussbücher*, ed. Schmitz, p. 448, para. 179. *Pope* no. xxix, an addition to *De auguriis*, refers (118-23) to other rites at crossroads still performed in Ælfric's day: *gyt* ('still now') *farað wiccan to wega gelæton*.

skili þa betr haldast oc væl hafast, oc vitu þer eigi þa hvessu mjoc er þer festa þa born sin oc sjalfar sic a hendi djoflenum, nema þer iðrist oc beri til skrifta.

And there are some women who take their children and go to the crossroads and there draw them through the earth for their health, and in order that they should get better and thrive, and they do not know how much they are consigning their children and themselves into the hands of the devil, unless they repent and make confession.

The ON version conflates the two OE passages quoted above and also includes details that are not given by Ælfric, above all the information about the intended purpose of the rite, namely, to ensure good health and prolonged well-being ('til heilsu þeim . . . oc væl hafast'). This information appears in the *Poenitentiale Theodori* and the Corrector (see n. 74); the writer (whether translator or reviser) of the ON text may have had a written source, but it is also possible that he was familiar with such a ritual among people in Scandinavia. As far as I know, no such ritual involving children is recorded in any other ON text, but there is an apparent parallel in the ritual of the *jarðarmen* by which adult men were sealed in the bond of blood-brotherhood, as described in some detail in *Fóstbrœðra saga*, ch. 2, and *Gísla saga*, ch. 6.[75] Both sagas agree substantially on the procedure, but the account in *Fóstbrœðra saga* is slightly more detailed and also condemns the ritual as a pagan practice later abandoned by true Christians. Long pieces of turf (one in *Gísla saga*, three in *Fóstbrœðra saga*) are cut in such a way that their ends remain attached to the ground, while the middle is raised to form an arch. The participants then pass under this arch, apparently undergoing a symbolic birth from the earth, which unites them as if they had been born from the same maternal womb. There can be little doubt that the ritual involving children was basically similar: the child is 'drawn through the earth' so as to undergo a symbolic birth from the earth, thus placing the earth *in loco parentis*, in order to ensure the

---

[75] See *Vestfirðinga sögur*, ed. Þórolfsson and Jónsson, p. 125 (*Fóstbrœðra saga*), and pp. 22-24 (*Gísla saga*).

continued well-being mentioned in the translation in Hauksbók. It is also implied that ill-health in a child was cured in the passage through the earth: for this there is a parallel in a folk-ritual current in eighteenth-century England in which a child was passed through a split tree-trunk to cure an infirmity, as recorded by Gilbert White in *The Natural History of Selborne* (1789), Letter LXX.

Anglo-Saxon beliefs about the power of the earth are reflected, admittedly somewhat obscurely, in a charm written down in the eleventh century (*Ker* 137: s. xi^1), which prescribes a ritual for improving and safeguarding land. Like the ritual of the *jarðarmen*, it requires the cutting of pieces of turf (line 4, 'feower tyrf on feower healfa þæs landes'); it greets the earth as 'mother of men' (line 69, 'Hal wes þu, folde, fira modor') and opens (lines 29-30) with a christianised variant of the widespread 'earth and up-heaven' formula,

> Eorðan ic bidde and upheofon
> and ða soþan Sancta Marian
>
> I pray earth and the sky above and the true St Mary.

This christianised formula also appears in a charm of uncertain function (perhaps against malaria) carved on a medieval rune-stick from Ribe, Denmark:

> iorþ biþak uarþæ ok uphimæn   sol ok santæmaria
>
> I pray earth and the sky above for protection, the sun and St Mary.

It is striking how Anglo-Saxon and Scandinavian sources widely separated in time and place coincide and supplement each other in these matters.[76]

---

[76] See *The Anglo-Saxon Minor Poems*, ed. van Kirk Dobbie, pp. 116-18, to which line-numbers refer; also, with different line numbering, Storms, *Anglo-Saxon Magic*, pp. 172-77. Moltke, *Runes*, pp. 493-95; partially quoted with further references by Larsson, 'Runes', in McTurk, *Companion*, p. 414. Wider aspects of these issues are discussed in Eliade, *Myths*, pp. 167-70.

THE OLD ENGLISH AND OLD NORSE TEXTS OF THE *PROSE PHOENIX*

(a) Introductory

Not quite in the same category as the texts discussed above, which occur together in OE manuscripts as well as in Hauksbók, is one other text that survives in related OE and ON versions, the *Prose Phoenix*.[77] The OE text survives in two manuscripts, both containing homilies by Ælfric, so that the *Prose Phoenix*, though not itself a homily, circulated together with Ælfric's homilies; one of these manuscripts in fact also contains part of *De falsis diis* (MS G: Cotton Vespasian D. XIV, s. xii med); the other is an earlier manuscript of Ælfric's *Catholic Homilies* (Cambridge, Corpus Christi College, MS 198).[78] The Corpus manuscript is mainly from the first half of the eleventh century, but the *Prose Phoenix* was added to the homilies in the second half of the eleventh century (Ker's dating); the two copies of the *Prose Phoenix* are thus separated by something like 70 or 80 years, which is reflected in their language. The Corpus text of the *Prose Phoenix* was apparently added to the manuscript somewhere in the West Midlands (perhaps Worcester, where the manuscript was annotated by the 'tremulous hand' in the thirteenth century), while the Vespasian manuscript was compiled in the South East (Canterbury or Rochester); the two versions of the OE *Prose Phoenix* differ in several details and are apparently somewhat removed from the hypothetical original, so the text may have circulated fairly widely; its provenance is unknown.

The *Prose Phoenix* is clearly influenced by Ælfric's alliterative prose but it uses some words of ON origin in a way

---

[77] An edition of the OE and ON prose texts was printed as an appendix in the edition of the OE poem *The Phoenix*, ed. Blake, pp. 94-99, which refers to earlier editions of the texts. An edition of both OE texts, 'Zum Phönix', in Kluge, 'Zu altenglischen Dichtungen', is of interest because much of the text is set out as verse (that is, like the rhythmic prose written by Ælfric).

[78] *Ker*, no. 48, art. 67.

that is unparalleled in Ælfric's writing; it was thus composed after Ælfric's time but while his style was still influential and, obviously, before it was copied into the Corpus manuscript in the second half of the eleventh century, so is probably a pre-conquest composition from the mid-eleventh century. The ON version is not in Hauksbók and is not preserved with other texts of English origin, but it appears in two manuscripts written in Iceland in the later middle ages: MS AM 764 4°, fol 1 (fourteenth century) and AM 194 8°, fols 7-8 (fifteenth century);[79] in each manuscript the text, a short account of paradise and the phoenix, is included in otherwise dissimilar descriptions of the world. All of this sets it somewhat apart from the ON versions of authentic Ælfric texts in Hauksbók. Moreover, the differences between the two extant copies of the OE *Prose Phoenix* show that copyists had handled the text with some freedom, in contrast to the striking consistency of many copies of Ælfric's works. The two ON versions also differ somewhat from each other, and it looks as if the original ON version was based on an OE text that was not identical with either of the surviving copies, and it underwent further changes before being copied into the late medieval manuscripts. This makes comparison less easy than in the case of *De falsis diis*. Norman Blake, who printed versions of the OE and ON texts in his edition of the OE verse *Phoenix*, was of the opinion that the ON *Prose Phoenix* is not a translation of the OE and that similarities between them are due to their independent use of a common, though hypothetical, Latin source.[80] The main piece of evidence cited by Blake in support of this view is that where the OE text has *cristal* the ON has *kristallus*, implying independent use of the same Latin source. The later OE text in Vespasian does indeed have the anglicised form *cristal*, but in the earlier Corpus text *cristal* is at the end of a line and the next line begins with two letters *lo* (omitted in

---

[79] See Kålund, *Katalog*, II. 184 (no. 1882) and II. 442 (no. 2407) respectively. The text in AM 194 is edited in *Alfræði íslenzk*, ed. Kålund, I. 4-6.
[80] *The Phoenix*, ed. Blake, pp. 94-99.

Kluge's edition): the reading is clearly *cristallo* (retaining a Latin inflection, as in the ON texts, but here in the dative case); this supports the theory of the original OE writer's use of a Latin source (he presumably used a form of *cristallus* with a Latin inflection, which was retained, with variation of the inflection, in the Corpus and Icelandic versions and anglicised in Vespasian) but it weakens the suggestion that the ON text is an independent translation from Latin. If one sets out the four texts concerned (two OE and two ON) beside each other, the verbal similarities are in many passages so close as to make any explanation other than translation unlikely, in spite of the time-lapse between the original and the extant texts of the translation (much greater than in the other works discussed above).[81]

Discussion of all four *Prose Phoenix* texts hitherto has largely concentrated on the significance of the Norse loanwords in the OE text: a study by Sara M. Pons-Sanz discusses this topic and refers to relevant previous publications, especially that by David Yerkes.[82] Two points may be made to supplement her discussion. First, she rightly dismisses Yerkes's proposal that the OE text is translated from the ON since it postulates an improbably early date (before the mid-eleventh century) for an ON literary composition, but she does not mention (and Yerkes also overlooks) that the wording of parts of the OE text is determined by the rhythmic-alliterative form used, which would hardly have been likely if it had been translated from a version of the extant ON text, which lacks this kind of verbal patterning. Secondly, she assumes without question that the ON text must have been translated in Iceland, presumably because the extant versions were written down in Iceland. I would prefer the suggestion, more economical in terms of hypotheses about the circulation of OE manuscripts and the existence of men capable of translating them, that the ON

---

[81] An initial comparison was made by Larsen, 'Notes on the *Phoenix*', 79-84.
[82] Pons-Sanz, 'Two compounds', developing points made by Yerkes, 'The Old Norse and Old English prose accounts'.

text that underlies the extant versions was translated from an OE original in England in the same milieu, even by the same individual, as the ON *De falsis diis* and other works discussed above, because the OE works translated are all preserved in manuscripts of Ælfric's homilies.

The *Prose Phoenix* is a short work, about two pages in Blake's printed edition, and it summarises a version of the phoenix legend broadly similar to that in the Latin poem *De Ave Phoenice*, generally ascribed to Lactantius (from which the OE verse *Phoenix* in the Exeter Book is translated). The OE prose writer may have worked from Lactantius (there are no verbal corresponences to suggest that he used the Exeter Book poem), but he probably used another unidentified Latin source, reflected in a few Latin words that remain untranslated: *cristallo* and *fons vite* and the puzzling name (in all four versions) *Radionsaltus* (presumably for *radians saltus*, 'shining grove'); Blake follows earlier scholars in postulating a single lost Latin source, which is highly probable.[83] The source was apparently an abridged prose version of *De Ave Phoenice*: it contains material that seems peculiar to Lactantius.

The relationship of the OE and ON texts may be determined by a short extract that is strikingly similar in all four versions. The Latin poem by Lactantius states (lines 153-54) that people assemble to venerate the phoenix and they make a marble monument showing its likeness and recording the occasion of its arrival in writing; the Exeter Book poem follows this reasonably closely (lines 331-35).[84] This theme of public veneration and the construction of a marble

---

[83] References to the OE verse *Phoenix* and the Latin source are to the excellent *The Phoenix*, ed. Blake, which prints the Latin poem in an appendix (pp. 88-92). Blake also includes (pp. 8-13) a useful summary of the development of the Phoenix legend.

[84] Lactantius 153-54: *exculpunt sacrato in marmore formam / et titulo signant remque diemque novo*: 'they carve its form in sacred marble and indicate in a new inscription the event and the day'; OE verse *Phoenix* 332-34: *gewritu cyþað / mundum mearciað on marmstane* ... : 'their writings celebrate it and they record by hand in marble ...' (texts quoted from *The Phoenix*, ed. Blake, my translations).

memorial seems to be original to Lactantius, indicating that his Latin poem, or more probably a hypothetical Latin prose derivative, is the probable source of the OE prose work. In contrast to this, all versions of the *Prose Phoenix* introduce an odd variant in which marble is replaced by wax, a change that is peculiar to this text and looks like a shared eccentricity, perhaps deriving from a rather peculiar handling of the unknown Latin source. The version in MS Corpus 198 reads:

> Ðonne wercað hio of weaxe, writiað fenix, metað fenix and hine mærlice þær wordum heriað (my transcription).

> Then they prepare some wax, write Phoenix, depict the Phoenix and praise him there gloriously with words.

The version in Cotton Vespasian D. 14 has:

> Ðonne wyreceð heo of wexe and writeð fenix and meteð hine fægere þær se madme stant. (*The Phoenix*, ed. Blake)

> Then they prepare some wax and write Phoenix and depict his beauty where the treasure (monument?) stands.

The author concentrates on the theme of an inscription but does not refer to any stone structure on which it was made, and he associates the act of writing with wax, although the text is uninformative about what processes were involved (Vespasian *madme* is a late form of OE *maðm*, 'treasure', but what it refers to here is uncertain).[85] The inscription is in wax but it is unclear whether the depiction of the Phoenix is also in wax or in some other medium, perhaps implied in Vespasian by the word *madme*. In the above translation I interpret *of weaxe* with some hesitation as a partitive construction in order to make sense of the extant texts:[86] this

---

[85] On the use of wax tablets for writing see Bischoff, *Latin Palaeography*, pp. 13-14; for Anglo-Saxon evidence, see Brown, 'Anglo-Saxon manuscript production', p. 113, and references there cited; cf. also OE *weaxbred*, 'wax tablet (for writing on)'.

[86] This kind of partitive construction is broadly outlined in Mitchell, *Old English Syntax*, I.508 (paras 1202-03); Pope has a detailed analysis in his glossary, s.v. *of*, section (l) (*Pope* II. 896); further examples in Godden's glossary, s.v. *of*, *CH* III 747; see also Mustanoja, *A Middle English Syntax*, p. 80.

construction is common after verbs of eating and drinking (as in *De falsis diis* 894-5, *he æt þa sona of ðære Godes sande*; see also the glossaries cited) but after *wyrcan* one might rather expect a direct object (such as *anlicnys*, as in *De falsis diis* 349-56), giving some such sense as 'they make [an image] of wax'; such a reading is in fact supported by the ON texts; perhaps a more appropriate direct object in the OE texts would be *breda*, 'tablets', describing the process of commemoration in writing. The reference to wax tablets (if that is the implication) does not correspond to Lactantius, but the writer may conceivably have been influenced by a development in late OE whereby *weaxbred*, 'a wax tablet (for writing on)', apparently came to be used of an inscribed tablet made of stone. Ælfric three times refers to the tables of the law received by Moses on Mount Sinai as *stænene wexbredu*, 'stone (wax) tablets' (*CH* II, 12. 135, 241, 250) and in *The Old English Heptateuch*, *Exodus* 31.18, the Latin phrase *duas tabulas testimonii lapidas*, 'two stone tablets of testimony' is translated as *twa stænene wexbreda*. The author of *The Prose Phoenix* presumably knew of this apparently contradictory usage and it may account for his reference to wax, although the OE text as we have it contains no specific reference to inscribed tablets; even so, the reference to wax, apparently due to a peculiarity of late OE usage, is common to all four texts and could hardly have been present in the hypothetical Latin source.

Both the ON versions supply a direct object for the verb and the wax apparently becomes a medium for sculpture. AM 194 8º (in Blake's normalised edition) has:

> Þá landsmenn göra ór vaxi ok eiri annan fenix ok marka sem líkast at öllu.

> Then the countrymen make from wax and brass another phoenix, and shape it into the closest possible likeness in all respects.

AM 764 4º has here (my transcription):

> Þeir [lanzmenn, *mentioned two lines before*] gera f[enix] or uaxi oc marka eftir honum sem þeir megu likaz oc rita nafn hans.

> They make a phoenix of wax and shape it like him as closely as they can and write his name.

The word following *gera* has an initial <f> but is otherwise illegible; AM 764 apparently envisages an image made of wax with an inscription, while AM 194 refers surprisingly to the use of both wax and brass; but all four versions agree, however implausibly, on referring to wax instead of marble, demonstrating the close relationship among them.

The ON loanwords in the OE text are obviously of interest: like Lactantius's Latin verse and the Exeter Book poem, the *Prose Phoenix* includes a statement that only God knows whether the phoenix is male or female. For whatever reason the author of the OE *Prose Phoenix*, whose English seems in general to be a reasonably idiomatic version of standard late West Saxon literary style, departs from normal OE vocabulary (as represented, for example, in the Exeter Book poem 355-56: *God ana wat ... hu his gecynde byð, wifhades þe weres*: 'God only knows what its sex is, whether female or male') and resorts to ON terms for male and (probably) female:

> and nafað he nenne gemacan, ne nan man ne wat hweþer hit is þe carlfugol þe cwenfugol buton crist sylf. (Corpus 198, my transcription)

> And næfð he nænne gemaca and nan mann ne wat hweðer he is þe karlfugel þe cwenefugel bute God ane. (Vespasian, in *The Phoenix*, ed. Blake)

> And he has no mate, and nobody knows whether it is a male bird or a female bird, except Christ himself (*var* God only).'

The author evidently came from, or was influenced by, a section of Anglo-Saxon society that had access to a form of ON as an alternative to OE; but the usage here is striking because the earliest recorded examples of ON loanwords in OE are generally words that had no exact equivalent in English, particularly nautical and legal terms, what Townend refers to as 'need-based borrowings';[87] whereas here one sees a further stage of development, later found in some Middle English dialects, where the vocabulary used may be regionally determined or a matter of stylistic choice. It is impossible to know whether the writer of the OE *Prose Phoenix* knew of an English alternative to *carlfugol* (*cwenefugol* is not elsewhere recorded: it could theoretically be a native OE formation, but is more probably an anglicised spelling of an ON word in this context); at any rate, these were evidently the terms that came most readily to his mind and furthermore they provide appropriate alliteration. One may note in passing that other formations on ON *karl* (*huscarl, butsecarl* and *carlmann*) begin to appear in English texts, especially the *Anglo-Saxon Chronicle*, about the mid-eleventh century, at the time when the OE *Prose Phoenix* was presumably being written. This use of one, probably two, ON loanwords in a late OE text suggests that the writer may have come from somewhere in the east midlands or the north; in thirteenth-century Worcester the 'tremulous hand' chose to gloss *carl(fugol)* in this text as *masculus* (Corpus 198, fol. 376v), presumably implying that, in that time and place, it was an unfamiliar word. At any rate, the writer of the ON *Prose Phoenix* clearly had no problem with this sentence: *En engi maðr veit hvárt hann er karlfugl eða kvennfugl nema Guð einn* (AM 194, in *The Phoenix*, ed. Blake; not in AM 764).

Comparing the OE and ON versions of the *Prose Phoenix* one can see the same stylistic feature as has been noted in *De falsis diis*: the ON vocabulary is more restricted and prosaic (compare below 31: 4/30, 35: 4/31 and 80: 5/14) and the rhythmic and alliterative patterning of the OE text is absent from the ON translation (a comparison that is difficult to make with the two versions of *De auguriis* because of the processes described above).

---

[87] Townend, *Language and History*, p. 203: he gives (pp. 201-10) an informative survey of the history of ON loanwords in English (pp. 201-10); the classic study by Serjeantson, *A History of Foreign Words*, pp. 61-103, is still useful.

The most economical hypothesis is that the same man, presumably a cleric who had access to a manuscript of selected homilies by Ælfric together with a version of the OE *Prose Phoenix*, perhaps a collection something like that in MS G (Cotton Vespasian D. XIV, which contains predominantly homilies by Ælfric with several later texts), but not this actual manuscript, which excludes *De auguriis* and much of *De falsis diis*, was responsible for translating several of these works into ON; or alternatively, among all the twelfth-century clerics rewriting and adapting Anglo-Saxon homilies, there was a group interested in evangelisation in Norway, including at least one Englishman with some knowledge of ON, who produced ON versions of what were then fashionable OE texts to further this end. The translations subsequently underwent varying forms of treatment by copyists in Norway and Iceland as they circulated more widely, so that many linguistic features of the original texts were lost.

The preservation of the OE *Prose Phoenix* in MS Cotton Vespasian D. XIV prompts a further consideration, for, as Ker noted (*Ker* pp. 276-77, art.54 and Ker's comment), this manuscript was in the late twelfth century handled by a woman, whose accomplished Latin annotations indicate that she was probably a nun. The intellectual activity of some late Anglo-Saxon and Anglo-Norman nunneries has been the subject of several important studies in recent years, so one should perhaps ask whether the translation of OE texts into ON, here ascribed to a monk, could have been carried out by a nun. There is of course nothing intrinsically impossible in this, but I know of no evidence to support it; on the contrary, the work is most likely to have been carried out at a religious house that had some kind of links with Scandinavia (most probably Norway): as stated above, such links may be found in some English monasteries, but I do not know of any English nunnery that had appropriate Scandinavian connections in the twelfth century, so this possibility must, at least for the time being, be shelved.[88]

(b) Comparative table of the Old English and Old Norse texts of the *Prose Phoenix*

The texts quoted are based on 'Zum Phönix', ed. Kluge, and *Alfræði íslenzk*, ed. Kålund. Some modified letter-forms in the latter have been normalised to facilitate reproduction; punctuation and capitalisation have also been modified throughout. Line numbers refer to Kluge, page and line numbers to Kålund.

CCCC 198, fol. 374v (extracts)	AM 194 8°, fol. 7r (extracts)
readings from Vespasian D 14, fol. 166r, in italic	readings from AM 764 4°, fol. 1r, in italic
(2) Paradisum nis naðor ne on heofonum ne on eorþan	(3/12) Paradisus heitir stadr sa er eigi aa himnum ok eigi aa iordu, helldr er hann i midio lopte iamnær himni ok iordu, sva sem hon var sett af gudi
(6) Paradisus hangað betwynan heofonan and eorðan wundorlice, swa hit se ealwældend gesceop	
(5) Nu is Paradisum feowærtig fædma hehgra þonne Noes flod wæs	(4/2) Paradisus er XL *fadma* hærri en Noa flod *var*
(7) Paradisus is eall efenlang and efenbrad, nis þær naðor ne dæl ne dune, ne þær ne bið snaw ne forst	(4/3) Paradisus er öll iamlöng ok iambreid, þar er hvorki fiall ne dalr, þar er eigi frost ne snior

---

[88] References to multilingual literary work in some English nunneries and their relationships with continental houses are included in Tyler, 'From Old English to Old French'.

The Old English and Old Norse *Prose Phoenix*

(8) ac þær is Fons Vite, þat is lifæs wylle

(12) þær is se fægere wuduholt þe is on bocum gehaten Radiansaltus

(13) þær is ælc treow swa riht swa bolt and swa heah þætte næfre on eorðan nan man geseon meahte

(14) ne feald þær næfre leaf of

(17) nis þær ne *hete* ne hungor, ne þær niht næfre ne cymeð ac a simble dæg; sunne þær scineð seofan *siðe brihtlycor* þone *on þissen earde*

(19) ðær wuniaþ on godes ænglas unrim mid þam halgum saulum oþ domæsdæg

(20) ðær wunað on an fæger fugol, fenix haten, he is mycel and mære, swa se ælmihtiga hine sceop, he is hlaford ofer eall fugelcynn

(23) ælcere wucan æne siþe se fægre fugol hine baþað in þam lifæs wylle, and þonn fleogeð se fugel and asett hine on þæt heagoste treow þe is on paradisum ongean þa hatan sunnan

(4/6) þar er brunnr godr, sa heitir lifs brunnr

(4/7) þar er einn fagr skogr ok dasamligr er heitir Radionsaltus

(4/8) þar er hvert tre rett sem kolfr ok sva hatt ath eigi ma yfir sia

(4/12) þar fellr alldri lauf af vidi

(4/15) þar er hvorki hatr ne hungr, ok alldri er þar nott ne myrkr, helldr er hinn sami dagr alvallt, ok skinn sol þar VII hlutum biartari en i þessum heim

(4/18) þar ero settir englar ... þangat skolo fara salur godra manna ok una þar til domadags

(4/22) i paradiso er einn fugl er Fenix heitir, hann er hardla mikill ok undarligr ath skepnu, sva sem gud skop hann, ok er hann drottinn yfir öllum fuglum

(4/25) hann laugar sik i lifs brunni ok flygr upp á þat tre er hest er i paradiso i gegn solo

(25) þonne scinæð he swa sunnanleoman and glitenað swa swylce he sio eall gylden, his fiðera syndon ænglas feðerum gelice, his breost and his bile beorht syndon, fægere and fage, *feawe synden swylce*

(31) hwæt, his eagan eþelice sendon swa clæne swa cristallo and swa scire swa sunnanleoma, his fet syndon blodreade

(35) Hwæt, se fægere fugol fleogeð of his earde, se þe is fægerlice fenix haten, witodlice wunað he on Egyptaland fiftene wucan fæste ætgedere; ðonne cumaþ to him, swylce hi cyning wære, fægniaþ and folgiaþ eall fugolcynn; hwæt þæt fugolcynn eall fægere fenix gretað, writigað and singað onbutan him.

(46) hal wes þu fenix, fugela fægerest, feorran hider cumen, ðu glitenast swa read gold, ealra fugela cyning

(49) ðonne wercað hio of weaxe, writiað fenix, metað fenix and hine mærlice þær wordum heriað

(53) fugelas ealle, fægere and fage fela ætgedere, feallað to fotum, fenix gretað

(60) and him an ræd hiow rudað on þam ricge

(4/27) þa skinn af honum sem af solar geisla, hann gloar allr sem gull, fiadrar hans ero likari englum guds, briost hans er sva fagrt ok nef, sem adr var sagt of fiadrar

(4/30) augu hans ero sem kristallus fetr hans ero sem blod

(4/31) enn þa er sa enn fagri Fenix flygr upp or paradiso a Egiptaland ok er þa XV vikur; þa safnaz til hans allz kyns fuglar ok syngia um hann á hveria lund

(5/1) kom heill Fenix hingat til landz, þu gloar allr sem gull rautt, allra fugla ertu konungr

(5/3) þa giera landzmenn or vaxi ok eiri annan Fenix ok marka sem likazt ath öllo

(5/4) allir fuglar falla til fota honum ok tigna hann

(5/6) rauð rönd liggr eptir baki honum endilöngu

(62) hwæt, þes fugol ferde *eft* fægere to his lande ymbe fiftene wucan, fugelas manige, eall embuton efne ferdon, ufene and neoþone and on ælce healfe	(5/7) þa er XV vikur ero lidnar, ferr enn fagri Fenix aptr til paradisar, allir fuglar fliuga med honum, sumir fyrir nedan hann, en sumir fyrir ofan ok a hvoratveggiu hlid
(72) and þæt fugelcynn eall ferdon heom hamweard, ælc to his earde	(5/11) þa ferr hverr til sins heima
(80) þynceð him þæt he forealdod sy, and gaderað þonne ofer eall paradysum togædere ealle þa deorwurðan bogas and macað mycelne heap togædere, and þurh godes mihte se hate sunne scineþ, and þurh þara sunnan hatnesse and hire lioman se heap wyrðeð onæled þe he, se halga fugol fenix, geworht hafað,	(5/14) þa var Fenix gamall vordinn, ok þa safnar hann ser fuglalidi miclu ath bera saman vidköst mikin, en af guds vilia vard sva, þa er sol skein a vidköstin, ok af hita solarinnar kom elldr i vidköstin,
(83) he feallað þonne onmidd þæt fyr and wyrðaþ forbærned eall to duste, ðonne on þone þriddan dæg ariseð se fægere fugol fenix of dæðe,	(5/18) en Fenix fell ofan i elldinn midian ok brann allr ath ösku, en eptir á hinum þridia degi þa reis hann upp af dauda,
(87) and bið edgung and farað to þam lifes wylle and baþaþ hine þærinne, and him wexan oginnað þa feþera swa fægere swa hio æfre fæereste wæron;	(5/21) ok er hann þa ungr i annat sinn ok ferr þa til lifsbruns ok laugar sik þar, þa vaxa honum fiadrar sem þa er fegurstar voro;
(89) and þus a emb þusend wintra he hine forbærneþ, and eft forfæger ediung up ariseþ, and nafaþ he nenne gemacan, ne nan man ne wat hweþer hit is þe carlfugol þe cwenfugol buton *god ane*.	(5/23) hann verdr gamall um þusund vetra, þa brennir hann sik i annat sinn ok ris upp ungr, enn eingi maðr veit hvort hann er karllfugl eda kvenfugl nema gud einn.

THE OLD NORSE *DE FALSIS DIIS* AND LATER OLD NORSE WRITING

The ON version of *De falsis diis* and certain other works was presumably taken, as the translator intended, to Norway; what reception it had and how widely it circulated there is unknown, but traces of the ON *De falsis diis* may be detected in a number of later writings. It may be that further work on the provenance of these writings might throw some light on the circulation of the ON *De falsis diis*: there is no doubt that it later came to circulate in Iceland, but this need not have much bearing on the earlier history of the text. It should perhaps be emphasised that my concern here is not with common themes that circulated widely, but with specific peculiarities, especially verbal, that can best, or only, be explained by direct textual contact.

The most notable text bearing a trace of the ON translation of *De falsis diis* is the Guðbrandsdal episode of the *Legendary Saga of St Óláfr*;[89] this connection with an early stage in the development of the Óláfr legend suggests that the translation circulated in Norway, even though the story as narrated in the *Legendary Saga* also appears in several later versions of the saint's life written in Iceland.[90] This particular borrowing is important because from the same episode it appears that the translator must have produced a translation of the whole of Ælfric's *De falsis diis*, so that the version

---

[89] This is the version preserved in Uppsala MS Delagardie 8. II 4°, ed. *Legendary Saga*; all subsequent references are to this edition. The Guðbrandsdal episode appears on pp. 29-35. The manuscript and the composition of the *Legendary Saga* are generally thought to be Norwegian: see Pulsiano and Wolf, eds, *Medieval Scandinavia*, pp. 447-48 and references there cited. Earlier writings on St Olaf, discussed in *A History of Norway*, ed. Phelpstead and Kunin, pp. xxv-xli, do not contain the motif under discussion here.

[90] The later versions considered here are: (i) the version by Snorri Sturluson preserved in the Royal Library, Stockholm, MS 2. 4°, *Den Store Saga om Olav den Hellige*, ed. Johnsen and Helgason, I. 271-82; (ii) the substantially identical version in Snorri's *Heimskringla*, ed. Aðalbjarnarson, II. 183-90; (iii) the version in *Flateyjarbók*, ed. Vigfússon and Unger, II. 188-92. All references are to these editions; I have not taken any later versions into account.

extant in Hauksbók, which omits the last quarter of the homily, must be the result of later abridgement.

The story of Óláfr's subjection of the inhabitants of Guðbrandsdal and of their consequent conversion to Chistianity has been discussed by a number of scholars, who have pointed to features in the story that raise doubts as to its historical authenticity: the description of the idol of Þórr is said to differ significantly from other accounts of Norse paganism, biblical sources have been suggested for certain details in the story, the reference to the bishop's mitre is said to be anachronistic, and it is alleged that the author may have been influenced by the story of Þangbrandr's escape when the ground opened under his horse.[91] The Guðbrandsdal episode culminates in an account of the destruction of the idol of Þórr, a story of a kind common in early Christian tales of the evangelisation of the heathen.[92] The fact that the destruction of idols was an established motif in early medieval hagiography need not mean that such tales could not arise independently or that they must be fictitious, but their value (historical or literary) must be gauged in terms of the conventionality of the components and the use of identifiable sources. The story of the idol of Þórr in Guðbrandsdal contains in fact one peculiar element

---

[91] See Bang, *Om Dale-Gudbrand*; Nordal, *Om Olav den Helliges Saga*; Lie, *Studier i Heimskringlas Stil*; and the introduction to Snorri, *Heimskringla*, II. lvi-lix. The story of Þangbrandr is recorded in *Flateyjarbók* I. 424, *Kristni saga* ch. 7 and *Njáls saga* ch. 101.

[92] See for example Augustine, *De civitate dei* V. 26; Bede, *Historia ecclesiastica* I. 30, records Gregory's instructions on the destruction of idols, and also the story of the pagan priest Coifi in II. 13. Stories of a similar kind among the continental Germanic peoples are recorded by Alcuin, *Vita Willibrordi*, ed. Levison, ch. 14, pp. 127-29, and by Willibald, *Vita Bonifatii*, ed. Levison, p. 31: see Talbot, *Anglo-Saxon Missionaries*, pp. 12-13; Adam of Bremen records an example in the Low Countries (*Gesta* I. xi) and several in Scandinavia: King Olaf of Sweden and the temple at Uppsala (II. lviii), the English missionary Wolred who smashed an idol of Thor with a battle-axe (*bipennis*) in Sweden (II. lxii), Egino's destruction of an image of Frikko (IV. ix), and Adalward (from his name presumably another Englishman) who with his followers destroyed various idols: references are to Adam of Bremen, *Gesta*, ed. Schmeidler. See also *Heilagra Manna Sögur*, ed. Unger, pp. 367 and 370.

that points to the use of a literary source, thus confirming the suspicions voiced by earlier scholars concerning the unhistorical nature of the story. The climax of the story in the *Legendary Saga* is as follows:

> En i þui bili laust Kolbeinn guð þeirra sva at þat brast allt i sundr . . . oc liopo or mys or gulli þæira sva storar sem kættir være, oc æyðlur oc paddur oc ormmar. (34. 5-9)[93]
>
> And at that moment Kolbeinn struck their god so that it broke completely to pieces ... and mice as big as cats ran out of the gold, and snakes and toads and worms.

The detail that distinguishes this from similar stories (like, for example, the destruction of an idol of Þórr by Óláfr Tryggvason)[94] is that when the idol was broken, mice and other creatures ran out. There is a source for this unusual detail in patristic accounts of the overthrow of the idol of Serapis in Alexandria. The story is first recorded in Greek in the *Historia ecclesiastica* of Theodoretus;[95] but this version can safely be ignored for our purpose because of the relative inaccessibility of Greek texts in early medieval Scandinavia and because it contains no details that are not to be found in more accessible versions. The Latin version of the story of Serapis in the *Historia ecclesiastica* of Rufinus (XI. 23-24) can also be ignored because it omits the detail of mice running out of the idol. This crucial detail appears however in the story as related by Cassiodorus in his *Historia ecclesiastica tripartita* (LX. 28): *Cum vero ejus abstulissent caput, greges*

---

[93] See also *Den store Saga* I. 281, Snorri, *Heimskringla* II. 189 and *Flateyjarbók* II. 191.

[94] See *Flateyjarbók* I. 319-22 and Snorri, *Heimskringla* I. 317-18; this story has much in common with the Guðbrandsdal episode and may have been influenced by it. The weapon of destruction is similar in these stories: in Adam of Bremen (see n. 92 above) it is a *bipennis*, Óláfr Tryggvason uses a *refðr*, Kolbeinn uses a *rudda, kylfa* or *klumba / klubba*: the weapon may have been chosen as a counterpart of Þórr's hammer (mentioned in *Legendary Saga* 32. 10 and the other versions) so as to give the incident something of the nature of a duel between equally armed opponents. Compare also an anecdote in Lid, *Joleband og Vegetasjonsguddom*, p. 158.

[95] *Patrologia Graeca* 82, cols 1247-48.

soricum exinde cucurrerunt, 'so when they had broken off its head, flocks of mice ran out'.[96] The author of the *Legendary Saga* could have obtained this detail direct from Cassiodorus if he had access to that work, or he could have found it towards the end of Ælfric's *De falsis diis* (P521-71) if he had access to the OE text (including the lines *fela musa scutan of þære anlicnysse*, P551-52); or (most plausibly) he could have found it in the ON translation of *De falsis diis* if the translation had ever been complete enough to include the final part of the homily in which the story of Serapis appears. This in itself would not be sufficient evidence that the ON version had originally included the whole of Ælfric's OE text, but there is one further piece of evidence that the author of the *Legendary Saga* was familiar with the ON translation of *De falsis diis* and that he was prepared to make use of it to add colour to his narrative of Óláfr in Guðbrandsdal, and this in turn makes it virtually certain that the whole of the OE *De falsis diis* must once have been translated into ON.

To explain this more fully one may first turn to a point made long ago by Bang and later repeated by Sigurður Nordal and Bjarni Aðalbjarnarson (see notes 93 and 94 above). One reason given by these scholars for doubting the historicity of the Guðbrandsdal episode is that it contains a detail that does not agree with other records of Scandinavian paganism, namely the alleged offerings of food to be eaten by idols; it was further pointed out that this detail has a biblical source in the story of Daniel and the Babylonian idol of Bel:

> Erat quoque idolum apud Babylonios nomine Bel, et impendebantur in eo per dies singulos similae artabae duodecim, et oves quadraginta, vinique amphorae sex. (Daniel 14. 2)

There is indeed a general resemblance to the list of foods given to Þórr in Guðbrandsdal, *Fim læivar brauz ero hanum færðer hværn dag oc þar slatr við* (32. 13-15); but an important discrepancy is that for the biblical twelve measures of

---

[96] *PL* 69, cols 1143-44.

meal (*simile artabae duodecim*) the *Legendary Saga* substitutes five loaves of bread, and for this there is an explanation.

The story of Daniel and Bel is related by Ælfric in *De falsis diis*, following the Biblical narrative very closely, and the verse quoted above (Dan. 14. 2) is rendered accurately in OE; this in turn, with some minor confusion over the quantities involved, possibly arising from the miscopying of roman numerals, is accurately translated into ON (see lines 664-73 and H532-43 in the edition below). The three versions of Dan. 14. 2 (Latin, OE and ON) thus agree as to the food offered to the idol (meal, sheep and wine), but none of this explains the reference to bread in the *Legendary Saga*. The idol of Bel, however, is not the only recipient of food in the Book of Daniel and its translation in *De falsis diis*: Ælfric also tells the story of Daniel's sojourn in the lions' den, including an account of the lions' normal daily diet. The food given to the lions is listed in the Bible (Dan. 14. 31) and again Ælfric gives an accurate translation, but, as explained above (p. 53), he introduces a potential complication by rendering the Latin *corpora* with OE *leapas*, an unusual metaphorical usage, which the translator took in its normal sense of 'baskets' and expanded into *laupar brauðs*, 'baskets of bread'. That the two passages in the ON translation of *De falsis diis* are the source of the reference to bread as an offering to the idol in the *Legendary Saga* becomes clear when the two lists of food are set beside each other:-

| Dan. 14. 2 (food for idol) | Dan. 14. 31 (food for lions) |

similae artabae duodecim, et oves quadraginta, vinique amphorae sex (Dan 14. 2)

duo corpora quotidie et duae oves (Dan. 14. 31)

mid feowertigum sceapum, and him man win sealde six sestras ... and twelf sestras melwæs (*De falsis diis* 669-73)

twa sceap to bigleofan and twegen leapas (*De falsis diis* 859-60)

tolf sesteri vins oc sald miols oc .xl. sauða (H540-42)

tua laupa brauðs oc tiu sauði til fœslu (H660-61)

Fim læivar brauz . . . oc þar slatr við (*Legendary Saga* 32. 14)

One can now see how the author of the *Legendary Saga* draws on both sources: from Dan 14. 2 (or more probably from its ON translation in *De falsis diis*) he obtains the idea of offerings of food for idols, while from the ON translation of Dan 14. 31 he takes the items of his list, bread and meat; but he could not have taken these from the original biblical text, which has no reference to bread. There is no doubt that he worked from an earlier version of the ON translation preserved in Hauksbók, for nowhere else could he have found the reference to bread: the change of *laupar brauðs* ('baskets of bread') to *læivar brauz* ('loaves of bread') is an obvious slip that might have come about either by misreading or by working from memory. Working from memory might also have encouraged the confusion of the two lists of foodstuffs, taking the function of the first (food for an idol) and the contents of the second (food for lions but with the non-biblical bread).

Since the author of the *Legendary Saga* used a version of the ON *De falsis diis* for one detail of his work, it is more likely that he used the same source for other details than that he should also have used the OE text: that is to say, he may be assumed to have worked from an ON translation that contained the story of the idol of Serapis, although this story is missing from the unique text of the translation in Hauksbók. His use of material from this source is supported by the following list of parallels (some of these parallels are commonplaces, and considered separately they could have been arrived at in other ways, but taken together they support the use of the single known source demonstrated above).

Ælfric, *De falsis diis*	*Legendary Saga*
and þæs anlicnyss wæs ænlice geworht ... mid golde beworht and mid hwitum seolfre (P 527-30)	... oc mannlican, oc var þat allt gulli glæst oc silfri (33. 8-9)
Seo anlicnyss wæs swiðe heah on lenge ... and heo wæs swa brad ... and þæt hus wæs swaþeah swiðe heah and wid (P 531-35)	Oc er bæðe har oc digr (32. 10)
Heo wæs swiðe egeslic on to beseonne for hire micelnysse (P 537-38)	Oc man yðr ogorlect þickia hve mikill hann er firir ser (31. 35)
Þa wearð eac tobrytt se arwyrða Serapis (P 545)	at guð þeirra var fallet oc brotet allt i sundr (34. 7)
feala musa scutan of þære anlicnysse (P 551-52)	oc liopo or mys (34. 7-8)
þæt men mihton tocnawan þæt þar wæs musa wunung and nan godcundnyss (P 554-55)	Nu mega þer sia hvat guð yðar matte ... nu sa þer hveriar vetter er þess hava næytt, mys oc ormar (34. 19-20)

An additional source for the last passage quoted from the *Legendary Saga* (34. 19-20) occurs earlier in *De falsis diis*, deriving from Dan. 14. 26, *Ecce quem colebatis*: Ælfric has *Nu ge magon geseon hwæne ge swa wurðodon*, and for this the translation in Hauksbók has *Nu megut þer sea a hvern þer truðut* (835-37, H641-42); the lines in the *Legendary Saga* may be seen as a conflation (perhaps made in the author's memory without conscious intention) of these passages from the ON translation of *De falsis diis*, and perhaps also from another passage earlier in the homily referring to Old Testament paganism: *Her we magon tocnawan be þæn hæðenum godum hwilce mihte hi hæfdon ongean þone ælmihtigan God* and its translation, *Af sliku megum ver vita huert megin þau hini heiðnu guð hofðu við varn drotten er alsz er valldande* (533-37, H421-24).

One further parallel may be added, even though it involves considering a version of *Óláfs saga* other than the *Legendary Saga* and questioning the assertion that one of the revisers of *Óláfs saga* was influenced by the story of Þangbrandr's escape when the earth opened under his horse. The relevant passage does not appear in the *Legendary Saga*, which merely expresses Guðbrandr's surprise that the pagan gods allow Christians to mock them:-

> Oc er þat furða at hanum skal lyða at lasta sva miok var guð oc hui þorer slict at mæla; oc undarlect þikci mer er guð var hæmna hanum æigi. (29. 22-25)

> And it is strange that it should be permisssible for him to insult our god so much and that he dares to say such things; and it seems amazing to me that our gods do not take vengeance on him.

At this point the version in *Den store Saga* (presumably by Snorri) adds:

> oc er þat furða hvi iorð brestr eigi i svndr vndir honom er hann þorir slict at mela eða goð var lata hann lengr ganga.

> and it is strange that the earth does not break open under him when he dares to speak such things, or that our gods allow him to continue any longer.

The version in *Heimskringla* is substantially the same as this, as is also that in Flateyjarbók.[97] It was this reference to the earth's bursting asunder that was seen as deriving from the story of Þangbrandr. The possibility that the author had this story in mind cannot of course be excluded, but in view of the parallels in *De falsis diis* already mentioned there can be little doubt that the main impulse for this passage must have come from the lost translation of the final part of Ælfric's *De falsis diis*, which offers a much closer parallel than does the Þangbrandr story; here the OE text has:-

> and his biggengan sædon, gif him [*sc.* Serapis] hwa abulge, þæt se heofon sona sceolde afeallan, and seo eorðe nyðan mid ealle tobærstan. (P539-41: cp. also P549)

> and his devotees said that if anyone should anger Serapis, the heaven would immediately fall and the earth below would completely burst open.

The verbal correspondence of *brestr* (rather than the formulaic *jörð skal rifna*) and *tobærstan* emphasises the parallel. That the reference to the earth's bursting open appears in later versions of *Óláfs saga* but not in the *Legendary Saga* is a minor complication explicable as an accident in the copying process. The alternative hypothesis, that the later author (whether or not Snorri) expanded a version like that in the Uppsala MS by drawing independently on the same supplementary source as that used by the author of the *Legendary Saga*, is possible but to my mind less likely.

One may conclude that the author of the *Legendary Saga* inherited a story, perhaps historical, about Óláfr's triumph in Guðbrandsdal and expanded it with homiletic material, including the ON *De falsis diis*. Conceivably of literary origin is the expansion of *feala musa* to *mys . . . oc æyðlur oc paddur oc ormmar* (Snorri and Flateyjarbók omit the *paddur*). The additions are of the same kind as the expansion in *De falsis diis* of Ælfric's *mys* (447) to *mys oc lemendr oc maðkar* (see above p. 57) but similar details also appear in an unrelated

---

[97] See *Den store Saga* 272. 7-8, and Snorri, *Heimskringla* II. 184; *Flateyjarbók* II. 188.

context in *Heimskringla*, *Haralds saga hárfagra*, describing the creatures that issued from the dead body of the beautiful Snæfriðr: *ormar ok eðlur, froskar ok pöddur ok alls kyns illyrmi*.[98] In both cases (*Óláfs saga* and *Haralds saga*) the reference to snakes, toads and so on suggest the creatures of infernal punishment in early Christian writings, perhaps making a point about the diabolical nature of the forces involved.[99] Perhaps there is also a reminiscence of the snake-pits of ON heroic legend to aggravate the horrific effect,[100] though in *Óláfs saga* the main impression is of the ludicrous and contemptible nature of idolatry, a view that could have been learned from *De falsis diis* as well as from other sources.

If the argument that the *Legendary Saga of St Olaf* makes use of the ON *De falsis diis* is acceptable, then the date of composition of the *Legendary Saga* (probably in the years about 1200) is a *terminus ante quem* for the completion of the translation.

A knowledge of the ON *De falsis diis* may also be traced elsewhere in saga-writing. The thematic similarities with *Barlaams saga* have been mentioned above (p. 44), while it has also been suggested that the account of Óláfr Tryggvason's destruction of the idol of Þórr in Þrándheim may have been partly shaped by the Guðbrandsdal episode in the *Legendary Saga* (note 94 above), and it is possible that *De*

---

[98] See *Haralds saga hárfagra*, ch. 25: Snorri, *Heimskringla* I. 127; also in *Ágrip*, ed. Jónsson, p. 5.

[99] References to serpents in descriptions of hell are too common to need exemplifying: the imagery goes back to references to Satan as a serpent (Gen. 3, 1 and Apoc. 12, 9) and to serpents with reference to pain (Vulgate Ps. 57, 5, Prov. 23, 32); toads may have been added because they were traditionally supposed to be poisonous, and perhaps through confusion with frogs, which are associated with evil or misfortune in the Bible (Ex. 8, 2-7, Ps. 77, 45, Ps. 104, 30, Apoc. 16, 13). The collocation of *ormar* and *paddur* is common (see Fritzner, *Ordbog*, s.v. *padda*).

[100] Literary references to snake-pits in the Poetic Edda (*Dráp Niflunga*, *Oddrúnargrátr* 28, *Atlakviða* 31, *Atlamál* 59, *Guðrúnarhvöt* 17), the Prose Edda (*Skáldskaparmál* ch. 50); *Völsunga saga* 39 and *Ragnars saga loðbrókar* refer only to snakes, but a panel on the Oseberg cart shows both snakes and toads.

falsis diis may have contributed something at two other points in the version of *Óláfs saga Tryggvasonar* in Flateyjarbók.[101] The first case concerns a problematic detail in the *Þáttr Sveins ok Finns*: when Finn Sveinsson has overthrown an image of Þórr (using, like Kolbeinn in *Óláfs saga helga*, a *kylfa*), he burns it and mixes the ashes into a porridge, which he feeds to some dogs with the remark, *þat er makligt at bikkiur eti Þor en hann at sealfr sonu sina*, 'it is suitable for the dogs to eat Thor since he himself ate his sons' (*Flateyjarbók* I. 392). No story about Þórr eating his own sons is recorded elsewhere but one is forcibly reminded of the classical myth of Saturn, and it is possible that the saga-author is here thinking of *De falsis diis*, which not only records the myth of Saturn but also equates several Norse gods with their Olympian counterparts in such a way that the account of Jupiter, later identified as Þórr, follows the story of Saturn. The relevant part of the text in Hauksbók is as follows:-

> En hann Saturnus var illr maðr. hann drap sono sina alla huerrn sem borenn var oc gerði at mat ser oc at siðan ... en sa Iupiter var þeira alra rikastr hinna heiðnu manna. er sumir menn kalla Þor. (H162-6, 188-91)

Until a better explanation is forthcoming, the reference in *Óláfs saga Tryggvasonar* to Þórr's eating his sons is best regarded as a confused reminiscence of the ON *De falsis diis*.[102]

Secondly, the account of the idol of Freyr in Þrándheim contains several motifs, each of which might have been found separately in a number of places, but which all appear together in *De falsis diis*. The claim of the pagans that their god spoke to them (*hann talade oft við oss*) and Óláfr's reply that this was the devil speaking through the idol (*þess get ek sagde konungr at Freyr hafui ekki talat vid ydr helldr diofullinn*

---

[101] I have not attempted to take into account other versions of *Óláfs saga Tryggvasonar*, except to note that neither of the two episodes discussed here is included in *Heimskringla*.

[102] Something like this argument was anticipated by Schomerus, *Die Religion der Nordgermanen*, p. 94. I am indebted to Dr Richard Perkins for this reference.

sealfr: *Flateyjarbók* I. 402) may reflect a memory of *De falsis diis*:-

> þar sao þeir dioflar, er þa hofðu suicna, hin fogru manlikan oc flugu þar i þeim oc meltu þaðan við hina ormu menn. (H268-72)[103]

In contrast to these loquacious idols, the constant silence of Freyr in the face of the king's attacks, *Freyr þagde . . . en Freyr þagde þa enn . . . en Freyr bra ekki vid* (*Flateyjarbók* I. 402) recalls the silence of Serapis in Ælfric's homily: *ac he hit ne gefredde . . . ne he nan word cwæð*, 'but he did not feel it . . . and he spoke no word', (P547-48, not in the extant portion of the ON translation). The destruction of Freyr is also made the occasion for a euhemeristic explanation of the origins of paganism; euhemerism was of course familiar in medieval Scandinavia and is mentioned in the prologue to Snorri's *Prose Edda*, in *Ynglingasaga* and by Saxo Grammaticus,[104] but its appearance here in the context of the motifs just mentioned suggests that the immediate source may be the discourse on euhemerism in *De falsis diis*; in particular the following parallel (thematic but not verbal) may be noted:-

> þat skulu þer ok vita at madr sa er Freyr het hefir uerit mikils hattar konungr j Suiariki . . . en er Suiar vissa at Freyr var daudr . . . þeir kölludu hann veraldar gud ok blotudu hann langa æfui. [*Flateyjarbók* I. 403]

> Maðr var sa einn mioc rikr oc bio i œy nokorre. er het Saturnus . . . En þeir hinir heiðnu menn aller blotaðu hann dauðan. [*H. edn* 158. 10-11, 25-6 (H160-62, 199-200)]

None of these parallels is strikingly close in isolation, and some of the phrases discussed may have had wider circulation, but the cluster of motifs common to both texts suggests that the saga-author may have had the ON *De falsis diis* in mind.

---

[103] Another story about a devil inhabiting an image of Freyr appears in *Flateyjarbók* I. 337-38.

[104] On euhemerism in Snorri see Holtsmark, *Studier i Snorres Mytologi*, pp. 9-16. On euhemerism in general see Seznec, *The Survival of the Pagan Gods*, pp. 11-18, and the works there cited.

A further parallel may also be considered: the legend of St Martin was widely popular throughout Europe and there are several different lives of him extant in ON. The main source for these was the *Vita Sancti Martini* of Sulpicius Severus, which includes the story of how St Martin was tormented by devils who appeared to him in the form of the pagan gods, Jupiter, Mercury, Venus and Minerva, and whom he dismissed by making the sign of the cross.[105] One ON translation of this, *Martinus saga Byskups* I,[106] at this point replaces the Latin pagan names with the names of three Norse deities: *i like Þors eþa Oþens eþa Freyio*. A source for this would hardly be possible to specify if it were not for the fact that the translator embroiders on his source by having St Martin overcome the devils by naming them and shouting abuse at them: *Þor callaþi hann heimscan, en Oþen deigan, en Freyio portcono* ('he called Þórr stupid, and Óðinn a coward, and Freyja a harlot'). *Freyio portcono* sounds very like a reminiscence of the ON *De falsis diis*, which calls Venus, *er heitir Frigg a donsko* (H253-54), a *portkona* (H225). Much here depends on the weight one attaches to the epithet *portkona*, which is applied in the same way in *Clemens saga*: *En hann kveðr Freyiu portkonu verit hafa*, 'he declares Freyja has been a harlot'.[107] It is likely that the two hagiographical texts have some interdependence in this detail and that there is a common source in *De falsis diis*. The transference of the epithet from Frigg to Freyja is of no great significance (both goddesses are named at the corresponding point in *Martinus saga Byskups* III, *ed. cit.* I. 618, but without the abusive terms); Freyja was also occasionally confused with Frigg and alleged to be the source of the name of Friday, as, for

---

[105] *Sulpicii Severi vita Sancti Martini*, 131.
[106] See *Heilagra manna søgur; Martinus saga byskups* I, I. 554-74: see p. 569, lines 20-26; the two other versions of the saga printed in this edition lack the distinctive wording discussed here.
[107] *Clemens saga*, ed. and trans. Carron, p. 44, line 9. Substantially the same accusation is made in *Lokasenna* but the language is strikingly different: *portkona* is a later and more prosaic term.

example, in Geoffrey of Monmouth, whence it is retained in the ON translation, *Breta sögur*.[108]

Finally, a work among the *riddara sögur* may be mentioned: *Mírmans saga*, ch. 9, relates the hero's attacks on paganism and idolatry and mentions in passing the story of Daniel.[109] The version in MS AM 593, 4°, is of particular interest here:

> Hann gaf ok líf Danieli spámanni, þá er hanum var kastat í gróf með VII léonum ok sendi Abbakúc spámanni af öðru landi á einu augabragði með mikit brauð, ok gaf han dýrunum.[110]

The statement that Habakkuk carried bread is biblical (Dan. 14, 32: *et intriverat panes in alveolo*), but the idea that this was given not (as in the Bible) to Daniel but to the lions must surely derive from the ON translation of *De falsis diis*, with its unique reference to feeding bread to lions.

These passages reflecting a knowledge of the ON *De falsis diis* among some saga-writers suggest that the text circulated somewhat more widely than the unique and truncated text in Hauksbók might lead one to suspect.

---

[108] Geoffrey's source for this seems to be unknown; see Geoffrey of Monmouth, *History*, p. 125 (98. 281-82): 'colimus ... Fream ... ex nomine eius Fridei vocamus'; *Breta sögur*, in *H. edn*, p. 269. 17: 'Freyiv dag'. See also n. 19 above.

[109] See *Riddarasögur*, ed. Kölbing, p. 156. I am indebted to the late Professor Desmond Slay for drawing my attention to this passage; see also *Mírmanns saga*, ed. Slay.

[110] Kölbing prints *með nytt brauð*, but Slay points out that the MS reading *mikit* is not in doubt here.

CONCLUSION

The foregoing study began as a comparison of the ON translation of *De falsis diis* with its OE source and, beyond the basic fact that at some point a translation from OE into ON was made, there is very little of certainty that can be said about this. There are no hard facts known about the time and place of the translation.

Arnold Taylor, whose study laid the foundations for subsequent work on the translation, points out that 'both Finnur Jónsson and Jón Þorkelsson give it as their opinion that the homily [in Hauksbók] was of Icelandic origin', and he himself refers to 'the Icelandic author', and more recently Abram's wide-ranging study also refers to 'the Icelandic translation'.[111] The reasoning is obvious: Hauksbók was preserved, and perhaps written, in Iceland, and Iceland, far more than any other part of Scandinavia, is famous for its medieval literary activity. Nevertheless, the inference depends on assumptions about the circulation and availability of manuscripts of Ælfric's homilies and the value placed on them; there is no reason to assume that any of these factors could apply in twelfth-century Iceland, but all are easily met in England at that time.

One is inevitably dealing here with conjectures, but the circumstances outlined above ensure that one particular set of conjectures is more firmly based than others. The additional fact that there are traces of ON translations of two other OE works casts further light on the whole process, showing that the translation of *De falsis diis*, rather than being a unique and unparalleled phenomenon, was apparently part of a larger enterprise, and the nature of the texts chosen points to a probable milieu for this work.

The most likely explanation to emerge from all the evidence is that at some time in England in the twelfth

---

[111] Taylor, pp. 101, 108; Abram, 'Scandinavian context', p. 437; the isolated phrases that Abram finds echoed in the Norwegian Homily Book (Abram pp. 436-43) are difficult to evaluate: they could be fragmentary memories of things read or heard.

century, at one of the pre-conquest Benedictine monastic foundations that held a library of OE manuscripts and where work was in progress on the copying and adaptation of OE homiletic writings, a monk decided that a laudable religious purpose would be served by translating some homiletic writings from OE into ON. What motivation and qualifications he had for this task is unknown, but some knowledge of both languages and some contact with a Scandinavian religious house, probably in Norway, must have been involved. Presumably with the approval and permission of his superiors, but without obvious collaboration or instruction, he produced an ON version, perhaps linguistically eccentric, of selected texts, probably working from one manuscript containing homilies by Ælfric and some other related works. He chose two, or possibly more, works (at least *De falsis diis* and *De auguriis*) that regularly appear together in a range of Ælfric manuscripts, and at least one other text, the *Prose Phœnix*, which, although not itself a homily, is preserved together with homilies by Ælfric.

The original extent of the translator's work is unknown, but evidence for it appears in manuscripts later compiled in Iceland, or perhaps Norway and Iceland. The clearest testimony to his work is in Hauksbók, which contains a considerable part of his translation of *De falsis diis* and portions of his translation of *De auguriis*. The main reason to assume that the translation of the *Prose Phœnix* in two late medieval Icelandic manuscripts also contains remnants of his work is that the OE text circulated in manuscripts of Ælfric's homilies, but the translation also has a stylistic aspect (a relatively restricted vocabulary) in common with *De falsis diis*.

Whether this enterprise might also have included translation into ON of Latin texts that were available in the English centre concerned is a matter on which there is no evidence, but here again MS G (Cotton Vespasian D. xiv) prompts an interesting line of thought. This manuscript has attracted a good deal of attention[112] and Treharne has pointed to the Canterbury connections of some of the texts included in it.[113] Of particular concern here is the fact that some of these survive in ON translation: MS G contains not only *De falsis diis* and the OE *Prose Phoenix*, as already explained, but also two OE texts that are themselves translations from Latin, parts of the *Elucidarius* of Honorius Augustinodensis (discussed above pp. 23-24) and the Assumption Homily of Ralph d'Escures.[114] This suggests the possibility that the compiler of MS G had access to a collection of texts (works by Ælfric, the *Prose Phoenix* and the Latin *Elucidarius* and the Assumption Homily) that was also available to whoever was concerned with compiling a collection of works to be translated into ON. Unfortunately for this suggestion, the Canterbury connection of the two Latin works is not all that firm: the Assumption Homily was probably composed in Normandy long before its author became Archbishop of Canterbury and, like the *Elucidarius* (even if that was composed in Canterbury), it circulated widely so that copies were available over a wide area and a long period of time, unlike the more restricted circulation of works in OE; the ON translations of these Latin texts therefore need not have been limited, as the ON translations from OE were, to one particular time and place. As Conti shows, the extant ON translation of the Assumption Homily was clearly made from the Latin text, not from the OE version in MS G, and there is no firm reason to believe that a complete OE *Elucidarius* ever existed: MS G has only two short extracts, but whether these were taken from a more extended translation, or whether they were translated *ad hoc* for this manuscript, is unknown: there is no evidence. So there is no reason to link the extant ON versions of these two texts with England. The Latin pieces have their own textual history and a study of the

---

[112] See Swan and Treharne, eds, *Rewriting Old English*, pp. 31-34 (by Treharne), pp. 48-54 (by Irvine) and pp. 65-71 (by Swan).
[113] Treharne, *Living through Conquest*, p. 157.
[114] Conti, 'The Old Norse afterlife', and Treharne, 'The life of English', pp. 169-72.

manuscripts would be required for considering possible places of origin for the ON translations, whether in Iceland or elsewhere.

As for the works translated from OE, the suggestion that we are dealing with the work of one translator in one place seems to me the most reasonable deduction from the evidence available; different explanations are obviously possible but they are likely to involve multiplying hypotheses about manuscript circulation and the existence of people capable of producing an ON version of an OE text at a date when that would have been seen as a worth-while enterprise. There is some evidence to support the suggestion made here, but less to support any alternative interpretation.

A manuscript of his work was probably taken to a Norwegian monastery, where it (or a copy) was known to the compiler of an early vernacular version of the life of St Olaf; a copy (probably, rather than the translator's original manuscript) was used selectively by the compiler of the religious texts that underly the collection, now called *Heimslýsing*, preserved in Hauksbók; the same or another copy was taken to Iceland and circulated there sufficiently to become the basis of a text preserved in two late medieval Icelandic manuscripts, the *Prose Phoenix*. Traces of the translation of *De falsis diis* also appear in some later Icelandic writings, suggesting wider circulation of the work than might be deduced from the imperfect text in Hauksbók. In this way one can reconstruct a hitherto unrecognized chapter in Anglo-Scandinavian literary history.

Knowledge of the English origin of these texts that circulated in Iceland in the late middle ages had of course long been lost; it is a coincidence that later English writing also came to be known in Iceland in the late middle ages, and one writer has stated that 'the fifteenth century was very much "the English century" in Iceland', citing a wide variety of evidence to support this claim.[115] But the circumstances of

---

[115] Hughes, 'Late Secular Poetry', p. 215; see also *Miðaldaævintýri þýdd úr ensku*, ed. Pétursson, and Jorgensen, *The Story of Jonatas*.

manuscript circulation and of Anglo-Scandinavian contacts were very different in the late middle ages: it is to be hoped that the situation in the twelfth century justifies the kind of consideration that has been presented here.

AN EDITION OF PART OF ÆLFRIC'S *DE FALSIS DIIS* AND ITS OLD NORSE TRANSLATION

The OE text is edited from Cambridge, Corpus Christi College, MS 303 (MS C), following the normal conventions: 'insular g' is printed as <g>; æ, þ and ð are retained as in the manuscript; modern punctuation and capitalisation have been added. Occasional manuscript punctuation is unsystematic and has not been retained; in some places the scribe marks a long vowel with an accent <ó>, particularly in some places to distinguish *god* (noun) and *gód* (adjective), but the usage is infrequent and irregular and it is not retained in the transcription, especially as modern capitalisation in *God* disambiguates one potential difficulty that the scribe seems to have been aware of. The mid-twelfth-century spelling of this manuscript is somewhat erratic if viewed as a version of Ælfric's late West Saxon literary standard but may well represent the kind of text the translator worked from; the occasional use of <æ> instead of <e> in stressed syllables (in some OE words, but also once in the Latin name *Mærcurius*) is sometimes found elsewhere; the occasional use of <æ> in unstressed syllables, presumably to indicate a schwa, can also be paralleled in late OE (the fact that it became common in the writing of early Danish may or may not be relevant here). The use of <ð> in an initial position is more common in this manuscript than in many others, but the common OE distribution of <þ> (initial) and <ð> (medial and final) was never fully systematic. Departures from MS C are printed in italics: this seemed an appropriate method for a text edited from a range of manuscripts, but a slightly different editorial treatment seemed appropriate to the unique witness of Hauksbók.

The ON text is transcribed from Hauksbók, mainly according to the conventions used by the editors of the printed edition, retaining the manuscript spelling (including the usage of <u> and <v>), but conventional abbreviations and contractions are silently expanded without any typographical indication. Obvious mistakes and omissions have been corrected, usually in accordance with *H. edn*; such corrections are shown in square brackets. Numbers in the manuscript are normally written in roman numerals and these have been expanded using the regularised Old Icelandic form. Modern punctuation and capitalisation have been added. A complete transcription into normalised Old Icelandic spelling would not have been appropriate to this text.

The text of *Um þat hvaðan otru hofst* is generally clear and unproblematic and where the editors of *H. edn* have made changes I have normally accepted their reading; but in two places I have ventured to differ. At *H. edn* 157.31-32 there is a syntactical problem, discussed above (p. 55, referring to H128-30); a more difficult question arises in *H. edn* 163.23, where the manuscript is unclear. At the bottom of fol. 7 the scribe evidently omitted a short passage and then inserted it at the foot of the page, where much of it is now very unclear, though the last words are clearly (*toko*) *þeir daniel*; the text continues on fol. 7v, *hann oc kastaðu honum*, so some change is necessary (either *toko þeir daniel / oc kastaðu honum* or *toko þeir / hann oc kastaðu honum*). *H. edn* chooses the second alternative, omitting *daniel* on the alleged grounds that it is a mistake. The manuscript evidence seems uncertain here, but the contextual syntax supports the retention of the name *Daniel*, since without it *hann* would seem to refer to the king. I therefore choose the first alternative, so that H653-54 repeats H475-76.

The two versions have been arranged in parallel columns, on facing pages, to facilitate comparison; this may have the effect of obscuring the rhythmic structure of Ælfric's prose, but I doubt whether the translator was affected by, or even aware of, this aspect of the original.

The accompanying translations into modern English have been added with some hesitation: they are fairly literal, are aligned as closely as is practical with the originals, and make no claim to stylistic merit. Each translation, and especially that from ON, aims not only to present the sense but also to reflect in some passages the syntax of the original: the result may seem stilted and wordy, it is obviously unidiomatic, but some readers may find it of help in unravelling the original. It also reflects the awkwardness that, in my understanding, characterises occasional passages in the Norse original. In some places, as explained above, I have ventured to emend the ON text where it seemed not to make sense (even using the OE text as a guide to what the translator may have intended), but my translation occasionally ignores eccentricities of grammar (as at H268-69, *diofla er þa hafðe*, where the expected text would be **dioflar er þa höfðu*).

Text layout

The verso (left-hand, even-numbered) pages contain the OE text preceded in parallel by a modern English translation; the recto (right-hand, odd-numbered) pages contain the ON text followed in parallel by a modern English translation. The reader is recommended to concentrate on the central columns containing in parallel the OE and ON texts, and to refer to the outer columns containing the modern English translations only when it may help to elucidate the originals. The modern English versions are of course of limited value and should not distract from the reading of the original texts.

THE OLD ENGLISH *DE FALSIS DIIS*

Modern English translation

Behold, most beloved brothers, the divine scripture taught us the worship of one true God, saying in these words: there is one Lord and one faith and one baptism, one God and Father of all things, who is over all things and through all things and in us all. From whom are all things and through whom are all things, and in whom are all things; glory be to him, for ever and ever, amen. The almighty Father begot one Son from himself without the participation of woman, and through the Son he made all creation, visible and invisible. The Son is entirely as old as the Father, because the Father was ever without beginning, and the Son was brought forth from him ever without beginning, of equal power to the Father. The Holy Spirit was not born, but he is the will and love of the Father and of the Son, from them both equally, and through

Cambridge, Corpus Christi College, MS 303

Eala ge gebroðra þa leofostan, þæt godcundæ gewrit us tæhte þone bigæncg anes soðas Godes, þisum wordum cweðende: an drihten is and an geleafa and an fulluht; an God and Fæder ealra ðinga, se ðe is ofer ealle ðing and þurh ealle ðing and on us eallum. Of ðan synd ealle ðing and ðurh þone synd ealle ðing and on ðan synd ealle ðing, sy him wuldor a to worulde, Amen. Se ælmihtiga Fæder gestrynde ænne Sunu of him sylfum butan wifes gemanan and þurh ðone Sunu he geworhte ealle gesceafta, gesewenlice and ungesewenlice. Se Sunu is eal swa eald swa se Fæder, for ðan ðe se Fæder wæs æfre butan anginne; and se Sunu wæs æfre butan anginne of him acenned, eal swa mihtig swa se Fæder. Se Halga Gast nis na acenned, ac he is ðæs Fæder and ðæs Suna willa and lufu of heom ba gelice; and ðurh

1 [p. 307] Eala …

THE OLD NORSE *DE FALSIS DIIS*

Arnamagnæan Institute, MS AM.544,4° (H)	**Modern English translation**
Liufir brœðr, sua segia oss helgar ritningar huersu [ver] skolum a drottenn varn 5 trua oc melir sua: at einn er Guð oc einn er almennileg tru oc einn er cristinndomr; oc einn er Guð alz faðer, oc alz er gerande oc valdande 10 oc raðande.	Beloved brothers, the holy scriptures so tell us in what way we should believe in our Lord and it says thus: that there is one God and one universal faith and one christendom; and there is one God the Father of all, who makes and controls and plans all things.

---

1 Liufir [fol. 4r]   **3** ver] H om.

that Spirit are quickened all created things that the Father created through his Son, who is his wisdom.
This Holy Trinity is one almighty God, ever without beginning and without end. They are three in name, Father, Son and Holy Spirit, and they are not three gods, but these three are one almighty God, indivisible, because in these three is one nature and one purpose and one action in all things.
And it is better for us to believe truly in the Holy Trinity and to acknowledge them, than it is for us to speculate too intently about that.

This Trinity created the shining angels, and afterwards Adam and Eve as humans, and gave them power over earthly creatures.

And they were able to live together without death, if they never broke that one command of God.

ðone Halgan Gast syndon ealle gesceafta geliffeste þe se Fæder gesceop ðurh his Sunu, se ðe is his wisdom.
Deos Halige Ðrynnis is an ælmihtig God, æfre unbegunnen and ungeendod. Hi synd ðry on naman, Fæder and Sunu and Halig Gast, and hi ne synd na þry godes, ac hi ðry synd an ælmihtig God untodæledlic, for ðan ðe heom ðrym is an gecynd and an ræd and an weorc on eallum ðingum.
And selre us is soðlice to gelefenne on ðas Halgan Þrynnysse and hi geandettan, þonne us si to smeagenne to swiðe embe ðæt.
Deos Ðrynnys gesceop þa scinendan englas and Adam and Evan eft syððan to mannum, and sealde heom anweald ofer eorþlice gesceafta.
And hi mihton wunian symle buton deaðe, gif hi þæt an Godes bebod næfre ne tobræcon.

---

43 ac] LRSW ac, C and

En hann eigum ver at lofa oc dyrka,	And we ought to praise and worship Him,
firir þvi at hann skop hinn fysta mann Adam oc hans kono Evam, er ver erom aller fra komner.	because He created the first man Adam and his wife Eve, from whom we all come.
Guð bauð þeim boðorð sin at geta, oc sagðe þeim, ef þau gaum gefe, at þau skilldu fœðast oc fulla tru gera, oc fylla himinriki þann lut er englar tœmdu firir mikileti sinu, oc firir ofpryði, oc firir þer sakar at þeir brutu log við Drottenn varn.	God gave them his one command to observe, and told them that, if they paid heed to that, they would flourish and achieve full faith, and occupy that part of heaven that the angels vacated because of their ambition and excessive pride and for the reason that they broke the law against our Lord.

Then Adam dwelt so carefree in bliss, and no created thing could hurt him in all the time that he observed that heavenly command.	Ða wunode Adam swa orsorh on blisse and him nan gesceaft sceððan ne mihte, þa hwile þe he heold þæt heofonlice bebod. 65
No fire harmed him, even though he stepped on it with his feet, and no water could drown him, even though he ran heedlessly in the waves.	Him ne derode nan fyr, þeah ðe he mid fotum on 70 stope, ne nan wæter ne mihte þone man adræncan, þeah ðe he on yðum urne færlice.
And no wild animal could, and no kind of serpent dared, hurt that man with the bite of its mouth.	Ne nan wildeor ne mihte, 75 ne nan wyrmcyn ne dorste, derien ðan men mid his muðes slite.
No hunger or thirst, no grievous cold, and no intense heat or sickness on earth could afflict Adam, as long as he faithfully observed that little command.	Ne hunger ne ðurst, ne hefigtime cyle, ne nan 80 swiðlic hæte ne seocness ne mihton Adam geswæncan on ðan earde, ða hwile þe he þæt lytle bebod mid geleafan geheold. 85
Afterwards, when he had sinned and broken God's command, then he lost that happiness and lived in hardship, so that lice and fleas boldly bit him, whom	Eft ða ða he agylt hæfde and Godes bebod tobræc, þa forleas he þa gesælða and on geswincum leofode, swa þæt hine biton lys 90 bealdlice and flean, þone þe

---

89 geswincum] *sic* LRSW, C geswicum

En þa er slict lif var Adame skapat, oc þeim hiunum baðom sua at þau skylldu ecki erfeði drygia, fyst þa stund er þau gettu boðorða Guðs, þa matte þeim ecki at angre verða.	And such a way of life was prepared for Adam, and for both of them, that they would not suffer hardship during the time that they held God's commands, and then no sorrow could befall them.
Eigi brunnu þau, þo at þau gengi i eld brennanda; eigi sucku þau, [þo] at þau gengi a se.	They did not get burnt, even though they walked on burning fire, they did not sink if they walked on the sea.
Eigi grandaðe þeim, þo at þau ormar hyggi; eigi sakaðe þau, þo at þau dyr biti.	It did not harm them, even though serpents stung them, it did not injure them if animals bit them.
Huarke var þeim at meini hungr ne þorsti, heitt nema kalt huarke kostaðe þau, meðan þau gerðu sua sem þeim hafðe Guð boðet.	Neither was hunger or thirst any trouble to them, heat and cold did not hurt them, while they did as God had commanded them.
Þa geck hinn flerðarfulli fiandi i ofund við þau beði hiun, sem hann gerir nu við oss alla siðan, firir þui at hann vill alla þioð suickia til heluitis, sua sem hann sueic þau beði hiun at þau brutu boðorð Guðs.	Then the deceitful devil went in envy of them both, as he now does against us all ever since, because he wishes to betray all people to the pains of hell, just as he betrayed those two so that they broke God's command.
En þegar er þau hofðu brotet þat, þa skilldu þau lata af þeiri hinni miclu selo oc lifa við vil oc við erfeði.	And as soon as they had broken it, then they had to leave behind their great bliss and live in misery and in hardship.

(lines 30, 35, 40, 45, 50, 55)

formerly the dragon dared not even touch.	ær ne dorste se draca furðon hreppan.	
He had to take care against water and against fire and to watch carefully that he did not fall down hard, and to toil for food with his own labour;	He moste ða warnian wið wæter and wið fyr and behealdan wærlice þæt he hearde ne feolle, and mid agenum geswynce him ætes tilian; and þa	95
and he had to preserve the natural virtues that God created for him, if he wished to keep them, with great care, just as good men still do, who with hardship hold themselves against sins.	gecyndelican gód þe him God on gesceop he moste þa healdan, gif he hi habban wolde, mid micelre gymene, swa swa gyt doþ þa gódan, þe mid geswince healdað hi sylfe wið leahtras.	100 105
Likewise the sun and indeed the moon were deprived of their pleasant brightness after Adam's sin, not on account of their own actions.	Eac swilce seo sunne and soðlice se mona wurdon benæmede heora winsuman beorhtnesse æfter Adames gylte, na be agenum gewyrhtum.	110
The sun was seven times brighter before man sinned, and the moon was as bright as the sun is as it now shines on us.	Be seofonfealdum wæs seo sunne ða beorhtre ærðan se man agylte, and se mona hæfde ðære sunnan beorht- nesse, swa swa heo scinð nu ús.	115
Nevertheless, after the day of judgement they shall have	Hi sceolon eft swaðeah æfter domesdæge habban be	120

---

94 He [p. 308]

60	Oc þa skilldu þau beði varna við elldi oc við vatne, oc þo matto þau varl[ig]a halda sic oc sin born sua at þeim i cne [eigi] felli,	And then they both had to avoid fire and water, and they and their children had to behave carefully so that they did not fall on their knees,
65 70	en þat er at þau brutu Guðs boðorð. Mikit gerði Adamr oc þau beði hiun oss ollum, firir þui at nu er heimr þessi morgum lutum verri en fyrst var hann skapaðr af þeira misgerningum er þau hiun gerðu.	and that was because they broke God's command. It was a great thing that Adam, and both of them together, did for us all, because this world is now in many respects worse than when it was first created because of the misdeeds that they both did.
75	Firir þui at þa var sol sjau lutum biartare en nu er hon, oc tungl var fyst sua liost sem nu er sol, til þess er Adamr bra af þui sem Guð bauð honum. En þat verðr eftir domadag er þau skolu iamlios vera	Because the sun then was seven times brighter than it is now, and the moon was at first as bright as the sun is now, until Adam disregarded what God had commanded him. But it will come about after doomsday that both the sun

---

70 misgerningum [fol. 4v]

to the full their brightness, just as they were created,	fullan heora beorhtnysse, be ðan ðe hi gesceapene wæron;	
and the moon will not grow old after that day and will be shining undiminished, just as the sun does now.	and se mona ne ealdað æfter ðam dæge ac bið ansund scinende, swa swa seo sunne deð nu.	125
Men can also earn with great hardship that they always dwell with God in joy after doomsday, ever without death, those who obey his behests laboriously; and those whom God despises will be sunk in hell in eternal punishmeant and endless suffering.	Men magon eac geearnian mid mycelre earfoðnesse þæt hi wunion mid Gode on wynsumnysse æfre æfter domesdæge, a butan deaðe, þa þe nu gehyrsumiað his hæsum mid weorce; and ða ðe God forseoð beoð besencte on helle on ðan ecum witum and endeleasum cwylmingum.	130

135 |
| Now we do not read in the scriptures that anyone practised heathen worship in all the time before Noah's flood, | Nu ne ræde we on bocum þæt man arærde hæðengild on eallum þan fyrste ær Noes flode, | 140 |

---

130 earfoðnesse] C earðfoðnesse

80	beði sol [oc] tungl sem þau voro fyst;	and the moon will be as bright as they first were;
	oc verðr þat at tungl þuerr ecki oc stendr fullt iafnan.	and it will happen that the moon will not wane but will remain equally full.
85	Ver megom nu með orðe oc með verki oc með erfeði varo oc olmoso til þess gera, at ver skilldum með Guði vera oc með hans helgum monnum i liose oc i fagnaðe, er ver heðan forum, ef ver vilium Guðs vilia gera.	Now with our words and works and labour and good deeds we can bring it about that we should be with God and with his saints in light and in joy when we depart hence, if we will perform God's will.
90		
95	Sva segia oss heilagar bœcr at engi maðr skal blota heiðnar vettir firir þui at þat gerðu menn firir Noa flod; en af þui varð su hin micla flod at Guð vildi firirfarast lata alt þat hit synduga folk af þeira misgerningum er þeir gerðu i hordome oc flimsku oc i meineiðum, i mutu oc i manndrape, firir vttan Noa oc sono hans þria oc þeira fiorar konor, þanan reis fyst sa villudomr oc utru fra þeim monnum hinum miclu er forðum varo.	Holy scriptures tell us that no man may worship heathen gods because that is what men did before Noah's flood; and therefore the great flood happened, as God wished to have everything destroyed that sinful people [had caused] by the misdeeds that they committed, with adultery and mockery and perjury, with bribery and murder, but not Noah and his three sons and their four wives; from all this first arose error and unbelief among those great men of former times.
100		
105		

---

105 oc þeira] *duplicated and corrected*

until the giants made the wonderful tower after Noah's flood	oððet þa entas worhton þone wundorlican stypel æfter Noes flode,	145
and God there gave them as many languages as there were workers.	and him swa fela gereorda God ðær forgeaf swa ðæra wyrhtena wæs.	
When they scattered to various lands and mankind then increased, then they were deceived by the old devil who had formerly betrayed Adam, so that they perversely made gods for themselves, and they despised the Creator who shaped them as men.	Ða ða hi toferdon to fyrlenum landum and mancyn ða weox, ða wurdon hi bepæhte þurh þone ealdan deofol þe Adam ær beswac, swa ðæt hi worhton wolice him godas and þone Sceppend forsawon þe hi gesceop to mannum.	150

155 |
| They considered it wisdom that they honoured as gods for themselves the sun and the moon for their shining brightness, and they offered them sacrifices and abandoned their | Hi namon þa to wisdome þæt hi wurðedon him for godas þa sunnan and þone monan for heora scinendan beorht-nesse, and him lac offredon and forleton heora | 160

165 |

110	Þeir toko til oc leta gera stopul or griote sua hafan at þeir vildu með þui koma i himiriki. En þa sa Drottenn var mikileti þeira, oc kom	They set to and made a tower of stone so high that they wished to get to heaven with it. But then the Lord saw their pride, and came there himself
115	þar sialfr er þeir varo er þa gerning skildu gera, oc uilti sua firir þeim at engi uissi huat annar sagðe eða gerði. En þeir menn voro tueir oc	where the people were who should do that work, and so misled them that no one knew what the other was saying or doing. And there were seventy-
120	siautigir. En af þvi ero nu sua margar tungur i þessum heimi. En þeir menn aller er þa voro vrðu sua vsattir at huerr þeira for a sins	two men, and for that reason there are now that many languages in this world. And all those men who were there became so quarrelsome that
125	vegar. En su gerning fell oll niðr. Þa foro þeir til ymisa landa en [mannkyn] vox þa [æfar] oc varð suikit af hinum	each of them went off on his own way. And that building completely fell down. Then they went to various lands, but mankind increased greatly and
130	sama diofli er Adam sueic fyrr, sua at þeir gerðu ser guð oc sao eigi skynsemdar augum a varn Drottenn er þa skop.	was betrayed by the same devil who had previously betrayed Adam, so that they made gods for themselves and did not look with understanding on our Lord who created them.
135	Sumir blotaðu sol, sumir mana,	Some worshipped the sun, some the moon,

---

110 Þeir *margin* Babilon
128 mannkyn...æfar] mannyni vox þa ofund *emended from OE*
132 eigi... **133** augum] eigi skyn *inserted*, semdar augum *above*

Creator. Some men also said concerning the shining stars that they were gods and they honoured them eagerly. Some believed in fire for its sudden burning, some also in water, and they honoured them as gods; some in the earth because it feeds all things.

But they could have known, if they had understood the distinction, that he alone is God who created all those things for the enjoyment of us men for his great goodness. Those created things do as their Creator appointed for them, and they can do nothing without the Lord's will, because there is no creator except the one true God, and we honour him with sure belief, saying with mouth and with inward conviction of the mind that he is the one God who created all things.

Yet the heathens did not wish to be restricted to so few gods, but began to honour as gods various giants, and men who were powerful in worldly affairs

Scyppend. Sume men eac sædan be ðan scinendan steorran þæt hi godes wæron and wurðodon hi georne. Sum hi gelefdon on fyr for his færlican bryne, sume eac on wæter, and wurðodon hi for godes; sume on ða eorðan for ðan ðe heo ealle þing afet.

Ac hi mihton tocnawan, gif hi cuðon þæt gescead, þæt se is ana God þe hi ealle gesceop us mannum to brice for his micclan godnesse.
Þas gesceafta doð swa swa him gedihte heora Sceppend, and ne magon naht don butan Drihtnes willan for ðan ðe na scyppend nis buton se an soða God, and we hine wurðiað mid gewissum geleafan, cweðenne mid muðe and mid modes incundnesse þæt se is ana God ðe ealle ðing gesceop.
Gyt ða ða hæðenan noldon beon gehealdene on swa feawum godum ac fengon to wurðigenne mislice entas and men him to godum, þa ðe mihtige wæron on woruldlicum geðincðum

	sumir stiornur, sumir æld, sumir vatn,	some the stars, some fire, some water, some the earth: they worshipped the latter because everything whatever is nourished by it; water because everything would die without it, and fire because it is warm to sit by; and the sun and all the stars of the heavens because from them come all the light in this world.
140	sumir iorð; firir þui blotaðu þeir hana at þar fœðist huatvetna við hana; firir þui vatn at alt mindi dœyia ef þat veri eigi; firir þui æld at hann er varmr við at sitia;	
145	en af þui sol oc oll himin tungl at þaðan kemr lios alt i heim þenna.	
	En þeir mattu þat uita, ef þeir vildi at þui hyggia at sa	But they could have known, if they had cared to think about it, that he alone is God who created everything for the benefit of men.
150	er einn Guð er þat alt skop monnum til hialpar.	

	Enda fengu þeir enn meiri villudom, oc blotaðu menn þa er rikir oc ramir varo i	Moreover, they adopted a greater error and worshipped men who had been powerful and mighty in this world after they had died, and thought that they would be capable of
155	þessum heimi siðan er þeir voro dauðir, oc hugðu þat at þeir mindu orka	

148 uita] eigi uita *emended from* OE

and awe-inspiring in life, although they lived foully.	and egefulle on life, þeah ðe hi leofodon fullice.
There was one man named Saturn living on the island of Crete, so mighty and cruel that he devoured his sons when they were born, and in an unfatherly manner made their flesh his food.	An man wæs eardigenne on ðan iglande Creta Saturnus gehaten, swyðlic and wælhreow, swa þæt he abat his sunus, þa þa hi geborene wæron, and unfæderlice macode heora flæsc him to mete.
However, he left one alive, although he had previously devoured his brothers; he was named Jove, evil and perverse.	He læfde swaþeah enne to life, þeah ðe he abite his gebroðra on ær; se wæs Iouis gehaten, hetol and *þwyrlic*.
He drove his father out of the foresaid island and would have killed him if he had come to him.	He afligde his fæder of ðan foresædan iglande, and wolde hine acwellan, gif he him come to.
This Jove was so extremely depraved that he took his sister as his wife;	Se Iouis wæs swa swiðe gal þæt he on his swuster gewifode;
she was named Juno, a very exalted goddess; their daughters were called Minerva and Venus; then the father foully lay with both and wickedly defiled many of his kinswomen.	seo wæs gehaten Iuno, swiðe healic gyden; heora dohtra wæron *gehaten* Minerua and Uenus; þa forlæg se fæder fullice buta and manega his magan manlice gewæmde.
These wicked men were the most glorious gods that the heathens worshipped and shaped as gods for themselves.	Ðas manfullan men wæron þa mærostan godas þe þa hæðenan wurðodon and worhton heom to godum.

---

204 Saturnus [p. 309]
215 þwyrlic] *sic* S, CLRW þrymlic 225 gehaten] *sic* S, CLRW omit 229 manlice] *sic* LW, CRS manfullic

iammiclu [dáðir] sem þa er þeir voro kuikir.	equally great deeds as when they were alive.
160 Maðr var sa einn mioc rikr oc bio i œy nokorre, er het Saturnus, en hann Saturnus var illr maðr: hann drap sono sina alla, huerrn sem 165 borenn var, oc gerði at mat ser oc at siðan.	There was one very powerful man living in a certain island who was called Saturn, and this Saturn was an evil man: he killed all his sons, each as he was born, and made them into his food and then ate them.
Einn let hann lifa en sa het Ioui[s], en hann var illr oc grimr	He allowed one to live who was called Jove, and he was evil and grim,
170 sua at hann rak foður sinn or œy þeiri er hann bio i, oc vildi honum at bana verða, ef hann metti taka hann. En sa Iovis var sua 175 quensamr oc daðalaus at hann hafðe systur sina at kono ser, en su het Iuna, oc gat með henni dœtr tuær: onnor het Minerua en 180 onnor Venus; þer baðar dœtr sinar hafðe hann at kono ser, oc hueria sina frendkono hafðe hann at skom oc cleke.	so that he drove his father out of the island that he lived in, and wanted to kill him if he could catch him. And this Jove was so lecherous and lustful that he had his sister as his wife, and she was called Juno, and he had two daughters by her: one was called Minerva and the other Venus; he took both his daughters as his concubines, and he treated each of his kinswomen shamefully and disgracefully.
185 Þa hina meinfullu menn oc hina fulu hofðu þeir þa at bestum guðum ser.	They adopted those wicked and foul people for themselves as their best gods.

---

158 dáðir] dauðir *repeated from previous line* **162** en hann] *margin* Saturnus **168** Iouis] ioui *deleted* iupiter *below* | var [fol. 5r] **174** Iovis] iupiter *above* **180** Venus] *altered from* vena (?)

But the son was nevertheless honoured more intensely than the father was in their foul rites.	Ac se sunu wæs swaðeah swiðor gewurðod þonne se fæder wære on heora fule bigæncge. 235
This Jove is the most honoured of all those gods that the heathens had in their error, and he is called Þórr among some people, him the Danish people love most strongly.	Ðes Iouis is arwuðest ealra ðæra goda þe þa hæðenan hæfdon on heora gedwylde; 240 and he hatte Þor betwux sumum ðeodum, þone þa Deniscan leoda lufiað swiðost.
His son was called Mars, he continually incited conflict and would always stir up quarrelling and misery.	His sunu hatte Mars, se 245 macode æfre saca, and wrohte and wawan he wolde æfre styrian.
This is the one the heathens honoured as an exalted god, and whenever they marched out or wanted a fight, they offered first their gifts to this god.	Þisne wurðodon þa hæðenan for healicne god, 250 and swa oft swa hi fyrdodon, oððe to gefeoht woldon, þonne offrodon hi heora lac on ær ðisum gode.
They believed that he could greatly support them in the battle, because he loved fighting.	Hi gelifdon þæt he mihte 255 micclum him fultumian on ðam gefeohte, for ðan ðe he gefeoht lufode.
A certain man was named Mercury in his lifetime, he was very deceitful and treacherous in his deeds and loved stealing and falsehood. The heathens made him a famous god and offered him gifts at crossroads and	Sum man wæs gehaten Mercurius on life, se wæs 260 swiðe facenful and swicol on dædum and lufode eac stala and leasbrednysse. Ðone macodon þa hæðenan him to mæran 265 gode, and æt wegelatum him lac offrodon, and to

En sa Iovis var þeira alra rikastr hinna heiðnu manna, er sumir menn kalla Þor; en sa var allr einn, en hann blotaðo menn a Danska tungu allra mest.	And this Jove was the most powerful of all those heathen men, and some men call him Þórr, for they are the same, and people among the Danes worshipped him most of all.
En hans sonr het Mars; hann vildi æ oc æ i illu standa oc i hernaðe oc i orostu.	And his son is called Mars; he wished to live continually in evil and warfare and battle.
En þeir hinir heiðnu menn aller blotaðu hann dauðan aðr en þeir fœri til orostu.	And when he was dead the heathen men worshipped him before they went into battle.
Oc hugðu þeir at hann metti þeim þa hialpa firir þa soc, at hann stoð i hernaðe, i morðe oc i manndrape.	And they thought he could help them in any dispute because he lived for warfare and murder and killing.
En var einn maðr sa er Merkurius het, en hann var sua farsfullr oc suika at hann for at flerð einni, at stela oc liuga.	And there was a man who was called Mercury, and he was so malignant and treacherous that he devoted himself exclusively to deceit and theft and lying.
Þann gerðu þeir heiðnu menn at guði ser, oc blotaðu hann at b[r]auta	The heathen men made him into their god and worshipped him at crossroads

(lines 190, 195, 200, 205, 210)

---

188 Iovis] *altered to* iupiter
195 En hans] *large in margin* Þór Mars Marcur*ius* oðin*n* ven*us* iofis doter **199** heiðnu menn] heiðin mann

brought sacrifices to him on high hilltops.	heagum beorgum him brohton onsegednysse.	
This god was venerable among all heathens,	Ðes god wæs arwurðe betwux eallum hæðenum,	270
and he is called by another name, Óðinn, in Danish.	and he is Oðon gehaten oðrum naman on Denisc.	
A certain woman was called Venus, she was Jove's daughter, so depraved in lust that her father and also her brother and many others had her in the role of a prostitute.	Sum wif hatte Venus, seo wæs Iovis dohtor, swa fracod on galnesse þæt hire fæder hi hæfde, and eac hire broðor and oðre gehwylce on myltestrena wisan.	275
But the heathens honoured her as a holy goddess and as their god's daughter.	Ac hi wurðiað þa hæðenan for halige gydenan swa swa heora godes dohtor.	280
Many other gods were variously found, and likewise goddesses too, with great honour throughout the whole earth to the destruction of mankind; but these are the foremost, although they lived in such a foul way.	Manega oðre godas wæron mislice afundenæ, and eac swylce gydenan, on swiðlice wurðmynte geond ealne middaneard mancynne to forwyrde; ac þas synd ða formestan, þeah ðe hi fullice leofodon.	285
290
The scheming devil, who is deceitful towards mankind, brought the heathens into that notable error, that they found as their gods such foul men, who loved those sins that please the devil, so that their worshippers loved their shame and became estranged from the	Se syrwigenda deofol, þe swicað embe mancyn, gebrohte þa hæðenan on þæt healice gedwyld, þæt hi swa fule men him fundon to godum, þe ða leahtras lufedon þe liciað þan deofle, þæt eac heora bigencgan heora bismær lufoden, and ælfremede wurdon fram ðan	295
300

273 Denisc] RS *insert P141-49*, CLW *omit* **301** wurdon] *sic* LW, C wurdor

215	eða gatna moti, oc a hestum biorgum,	and where paths meet and on the highest hills,
	en hann het Oðenn a donsku.	and he is called Óðinn in Danish.
	Kona ein var su er het Vena;	There was one woman called Venus; she was Jove's daughter,
220	su var Iofis dotter, en hon var sua manngiorn oc sua org oc sua ill at hon la með feðr sinum oc með morgum monnum, oc hafðezt sua	and she was so eager for men, and so depraved and wicked, that she lay with her father and with many men, and behaved as
225	sem portkona.	a harlot.
	En firir henni œrðust oc heiðnir menn ok kallaðu hana gyðiu oc sins guðs dottor.	And heathen men went mad for her [honoured her?] and called her a goddess and their god's daughter.
230	Mart var þess alsz er menn kallaðu guð	There were many more of this kind that men called gods
	vm allann miðgarð.	throughout the whole earth.
	Hinn illi diofull hafðe sua suicna þa hina heiðnu	The wicked devil had so deceived those heathen men
235	menn at þeir toko illa kalla oc argar konor, oc blotaðu guð sin þa menn er þat eitt gerðu er fianda vili var.	that they took wicked men and pernicious women, and worshipped as gods those people who did that one thing that was the devil's wish.

---

215 eða gatna] *written above alteration*

almighty God, who abhors sins and loves purity.

They allocated also to the sun and to the moon and to other gods, to each his day:

first to the sun, Sunday, and then to the moon, Monday, and they devoted the third day to Mars, their war-god, to please him.

The fourth day they gave as an encouragement to the aforesaid Mercury, their famous god. The fifth day they celebrated in honour of glorious Jove, the most famous god.

The sixth day they ascribed to the shameless goddess called Venus, and Frigg in Danish.

The seventh day they gave to old Saturn, the father of the gods, to satisfy themselves, but in the final position however, although he was oldest.

They wished furthermore to honour those gods more solemnly and they dedicated stars to them, as if they had control over them: the seven planets, the sun and moon and the other five, that continually go

ælmihtigan Gode, se ðe leahtras onscunað and lufað þa clænnysse.
Hi gesettan eac þa þære sunnan and þan monan and þam oðrum godum ælcum his dæg:
ærest ðære sunnan þonæ Sunandæg, and siððan þan monan þone Monandæg, and þone ðriddan dæg hi ðeowdon Marte, heora feohte-gode, him to fultume.
Ðone feorðe dæg hi sealdon him to frofre þan foresædan Mærcurie, heora mæran gode. Ðone fiftan dæg hi freolsodon mærlice Iove to wurðmente, þam mærestan gode.
Ðone sixtan dæg hi gesetton þære scamleasan gydenan, Venus gehaten and Fricg on Denisc.
Ðone seofoðan dæg hi sealdan Saturne þam ealdan, þæra goda fæder, him sylfum to frofre, endenexð swaðeah, þeah he yldost wære.
Hi woldon git wurðian arwurðlicor þa godas and forgeafon him steorran, swylce hi ahton heora geweald, þa seofon tunglan, sunnan and monan and þa oðre fif þe farað æfre

305

310

315

320

325

330

335

---

312 dæg [p. 310]

240	Sua var mannkynit suikit til þess er var Drottenn gaf þeim enga gaum.	Thus mankind was so deceived that our Lord took no heed of them.
245	A marga vega varo menn viltir sua at þeir gafo sol oc mana daga, oc oðrum guðum sinum:	In many ways men were so misled that they dedicated days to the sun and moon and their other gods:
	sol gafo þeir sunnudag en mana manadag	to the sun they gave Sunday and to the moon Monday
	en tysdag gafo þeir Marti.	and Tuesday they gave to Mars.
250	Hinn fiorða dag gafo þeir Mercurio, þann er ver kollum Oðenn.	The fourth day they gave to Mercury, whom we call Óðinn.
	En hinn setta dag gafo þeir hinni orgu Venu, er heitir Frigg a donsko.	And the sixth day they gave to the pernicious Venus, who is called Frigg in Danish.
255	Hinn siaunda dag gafo þeir Saturno, er var hinn ellsti faðer þeira allra guða.	The seventh day they gave to Saturn, who was the oldest father of all their gods.

---

253 Venu] *altered to* veneri

against the movement of the heavens towards the east; but the heavens continually turn them back. But nevertheless, the stars were shining in the heavens in the beginning of the earth, before the evil gods were conceived or chosen as gods.

They also made images for the gods they honoured and they designed them with skill, some of beaten gold, some of white silver, some also of stone, some also of various kinds of wood, according to their abilities.

And they built houses for them which they called temples, and inside they set up their beloved gods bound with lead and they prayed to them.

Then the devils who had formerly betrayed them saw the fair images and flew into them and spoke through the images to the
wretched people, and thus misled them with their lies and brought their souls to infernal torments.

Smiths made them cunningly with skill and often

ongean þone roder to eastdæle wærd. Ac hi gebigð seo heofon undærbæc æfre. Ac ða steorran swaðeah scinon on heofonum on frymðe middaneardes, ær ða manfullan godas acennede wurdon oððe gecorene to godum.
Hi worhton eac onlicnissa þam arwurðan godum, sume of smætum golde, and þa asmeadon mid cræfte, sume of hwitum seolfre, sume eac of stanum, sume eac of mislicum antimbre, be þam ðe heora mihta wæron.
And him hus arærdon þæt hi heton templ, and þærinne gelogodon heora leofan godes mid leade gebundene and gebædon hi þærto.
Ða gesawon ða deoflu þe hi beswicon on ær þa fægeran anlicnyssa, and flugon þærto, and þurh ða anlicnyssa spræcon to ðam earmum mannum, and hi swa forlæddon mid heora leasungum and to hellicum suslum heora sawla gebrohton.
Smiðas hi worhton smealice mid cræfte and oft

340

345

350

355

360

365

370

375

---

371 leasungum] *sic* LR, C leasunga **374** Smiðas] C smiðos

| | Þa gerðu þeir hinir heiðnu menn manlikan or rauðu gulli oc or huitu silfri; suma gerðo þeir or steinum, suma or stockum: gerði e huerr or þui er efni hafðe til. | Then the heathen men made images out of red gold and white silver; some they made out of stones, some of wood, each man always used whatever material he had. |

260

| | Oc gerðu þeim hus oc kallaðu þat hof þeira, oc settu þau mannlikan þar inni, oc baðo ser goðs til. | And they made a building for them and called it their temple, and they set the image inside it and made their petitions to the god. |

265

| | Þar sao þeir diofla er þa hafðe aðr suicna hin fogru manlikan, oc flugu þar i þeim, oc meltu þaðan við þa hina ormu menn, oc villu menn oc lerðu þa til þess er þeir komu salum þeira oc sialfum þeim i heluiti. | The devils who had previously deceived them saw there the fair images and flew into them and spoke from thence to the wretched people and led them astray and taught them so that they brought their souls and themselves into hell. |

270

275

Sumir gerðu manlikan með miclum hannerðum oc

Some made images with great skill and

---

263 er…hafðe] *altered to* efni er hafðe **269** hin] oc hini
278 miclum [fol. 5v]

sold the silver gods, one for a greater price according to how he was made, one for less according to his value.	gesealdan þa sylfrenan godas, sumne to maran wurðe be ðan ðe he gemacod wæs, sumne eac waclicor be ðam ðe his wurð wæs.
And as long as he worked on the half-finished god with his carving-tool and wickedly hollowed out its eyes, he felt no fear of the image; but when it was completed, he worshipped it as a god.	And swa lange swa he sloh þone samworhtan god and mid his græfsexe holode his eagan hetelice, ne stod him nan ege of þære anlicnysse; ac ðonne heo geworht wæs, he wurðode hi for god.
We read in the book called *Liber Regum* that the heathen Philistines were often at war with the people of Israel, who alone believed in the almighty God in the way of Abraham.	We rædeð on þære bec þe is *Liber Regum* gehaten þæt ða hæðenan Philistei fuhton gelome wið ðæt Israhela folc, þa ana þa gelefdon on ðone ælmihtigan God on Abrahames wisan.
Then on one occasion however it happened because of their sins that the heathens won a victory over the people and seized *Arcam Domini*, that is, the Ark of the Lord In the ark were kept the heavenly food and the rod of Aaron, the first bishop,	Ða on sumne sæl gelamp hit for heora synnan swaðeah þæt þa hæðenan gefuhton on ðan folce sigæ and *Arcam Domini* gelahton, þæt is ðrihtnes scrin. On ðan scrine wæs gehealdon se heofonlica mete and Aarones gyrd, þæs ærestan biscopas,

280	seldu með verði, suma við minna en suma við meira.	sold them according to their value, some for less and some for more.
285	Sva huern sem koma matte meðan þeir gerðu, þa þotte þeim gaman eitt at; en þa er gort hofðu oc þeir guð kalladu, þa stoð þeim age af oc voro aller reddir við þa.	If anyone happened to come while they were at work, it seemed to them amusing; but when they had made it and called it their god, they stoood in awe of it and were all afraid of it.
290
295	Ver hofum lesit a boc þeiri er heitir *Liber Regum* at þeir hinir heiðnu menn af lande þui er heitir Philistim borðust oft við I[s]raels folk, en þeir einir menn hofðu þa retta tru til vars Drottens, sua sem Abraham hafðe firir þeim aðr.	We have read in the book called *Liber Regum* that the heathen men from the land called Philistia were often at war with the people of Israel, who alone had the true belief in our Lord, just as Abraham previously had before them.
300
305
310	En þa varð þat i eitthuert sinn firir syndum þeira hinna cristnu manna at þeir hinir heiðnu menn hofðu gagn, oc fengu af þeim orc, þa er mikill heilagr domr la i. Þar la i vondr sa er Moysess hafðe, er var Drottenn sialfr seldi i hond honum; en þeim vendi laust Moyses a Hafet Rauða þa er Farao konungr for eftir þeim með sinn her oc vildi drepa þa alla; en þa stoð hafet tueim megim sem steinnveggr. En Moyses geck yfir haf þurrum fotum, en Farao oc lið hans for	And then it happened on one occasion that, for the sins of the Christian men, the heathen men had the victory and captured from them the ark, which a very holy relic lay in. In it lay the rod that Moses had, which our Lord himself gave into his hand; Moses used this on the Red Sea when Pharaoh the king pursued them with his army, intending to kill them all, but the sea stood on both sides like a stone wall. And Moses went over the sea with dry feet, but Pharaoh and his men went

and the tablets of Moses, which were inscribed on the mountain by God's finger to instruct his people.	and Moyses tabulan þe on þam munte wæron mid Godes fingre awritene his folc to lare.
Then the heathens brought the aforesaid ark with the heavenly relics home to their temple and placed it honourably before their god: this god was named Dagon, very dear to the heathens.	Ða feredon ða hæðenan þæt foresæde scrin mid þam heofenlican haligdome ham to heora temple and setton hit arwurðlice up to heora godæ: se god hatte Dagon, þan hæðenum swiðe dyre.
Early the next morning when they went to the temple they found their god lying on the floor before the ark of the Lord, as if he were begging for peace.	Eft þa on ærnemorgæn, þa þa hi in eoden to þam temple, þa fundon hi heora god on þære flora licgan ætforan ðan Godes scrine, swylce he friðes bæde.
After this they raised up Dagon over the ark of the Lord where he formerly stood and walked away.	Hi hofon ða eft Dagon to þan Drihtnes scrine þær ðær he ær stod and stopon him þanon.
They came back in the morning to find out how things were;	Comon þa eft on morgen and cunnodon hu hit wære;

Line numbers: 410, 415, 420, 425

416 dyre] *sic* LR, C leof
417 ærnemorgæn] ærne [p. 311]morgæn   418 to... 419 temple] *sic* CL, *not in* R

315 eftir þeim þa hina somo leið; þa laucst hafet saman en þeir drucnaðu þa aller. Þar la oc i orc þeiri stein- spiold þau er var Drottenn feck sialfr i hendr Moysi, oc 320 hann hafðe skrifat a log oll með bocstofum, er menn skilldu þa hafa oc nu i þessum heimi. Þar la oc i manna, en þat var fœsla su 325 er var Drottenn sendi or hifnum Moysi oc hans liði, er hann sendi þa fiorirtigir vetra i œyðimorc. Þa fœrðu þeir hinir heiðnu 330 menn þa orc með þeim miclum helgum dome, er or hifnum kom, til sins hofs oc settu vpp hia sinu guði: en þat kallaðu þeir Dagon 335 en yfir honum letu þeir heiðnir menn mioc dyrlega. Þat var einn morgen arla er þeir komo inn i hof sitt, þa fundu þeir guð sitt a golfe 340 liggia firir orkenni niðri, sem hann beði friðar. Þa toko þeir enn Dagon oc settu vpp i sama stað sem hann stoð aðr hia hinum 345 helga dome. Þa como þeir at oðrum morne at vita huessu þa	after them along the same path; then the sea closed together and they were all drowned. Also in the ark there lay the stone tablets which our Lord himself placed in the hands of Moses, and He had written on them with letters all the law that men needed then, and still do now in this world. Also in there was manna, that was the food that our Lord sent from heaven to Moses and his people, and He went on sending it for forty years in the wilderness. Then the heathen men carried the ark with the very holy relics from heaven to their temple and set it up beside their god whom they called Dagon, and the heathen people expressed great love of him. It was early morning when they came into their temple and found their god lying down on the floor before the ark as if he were begging for peace. Then they took Dagon and set him up in the same place where he stood before beside the holy shrine. Then they came the next morn- ing to see how it was

there was Dagon's severed head in the doorway and his two hands cut off on the threshold, and Dagon lay headless before the holy ark, because it was not fitting for the devilish image to stand so exalted beside the holy ark.	þa wæs Dagones heafod æt þære dura forcorfen and his twa handbreda aheawen æt ðan þrexwolde, and Dagon læg heafodleas ætforan þam halgan scrine, for ðam ðe hit ne gedafnode þære deoflican anlicnysse þæt heo wið ðæt halig scrin swa healice stode.
Then God in his wrath straight-way sent a sudden plague on that people and killed the Philistines because they had the holy ark among their idolatry, as if they wished to keep it.	Ða sænde God sona mid graman to ðære leode færlicne mancwealm and ða Philisteos acwealde, for ðan ðe hi hæfdon þæt halige scrin þær on heore heðenscipe, swilce hi hit habban woldon.
There came upon them also many mice throughout the land and laid waste their fields and destroyed the land.	Heom comon to eac mys manega geond þæt land and heora æceras aweston and ðone eard fordydon.
Then the countryfolk said that they would send the ark of God away throughout their five towns from shire to shire so that the plague would cease.	Ða gecweadon þa landleoda þæt hi lædan woldon þæt Godes scrin him fram geond heora fif burga fram scire to scire þæt se cwealm geswice.
They carried the ark throughout the five towns, and wherever it came, straightway came the plague and killed the Philistines with sudden death, and they wretchedly lamented this cruel death.	Hi feredon ða þæt scrin geond ða fif burga, and swa hwær swa hit becom, swa com se cwealm sona and mid færlicum deaðe þa Philisteos acwealde, and hi earmlice hrymdon for ðan reðan deaðe.

Line numbers: 430, 435, 440, 445, 450, 455, 460

---

429 wæs] *sic* LRW, C þæs

fœri; þa funnu þeir Dagon guð sitt i durum vti 350 hofuðlausan oc hendr af baðar,	going: they found then Dagon their god outside the door headless and with both hands off,
firir þui for þat sua, at eigi matte alt vera saman Drottens vars sendingar oc 355 diofuls manlikan.	it was like that because they could not be close together, our Lord's gifts and the devil's image.
Þa varp Guð reiði sinni a þa þioð oc sendi til þeira manndauða oc varan, firir þer saker at þeir hofðu þar 360 hit helga skrin i sinu heiðna hofe.	Then God turned his anger on that nation and sent them a deadly plague as a warning, for the reason that they had there the holy shrine in their heathen temple.
Mys ok lemendr oc maðkar a lande þvi ato korn alt firir monnum oc grasretr oc 365 viðarretr, oc firirforo landenu ollu.	Mice and lemmings and maggots ate all the corn of the people in that country, and grass-roots and tree-roots, and destroyed all the land.
Þa færðu þeir landslyðren þat hit helga skrin til annarar borgar fra annare, 370 þa var þar manndauði hinn mesti sem þat hit helga skrin kom.	Then the people of that land carried the holy shrine from one town to another, then the plague was worst wherever the holy shrine came.

360 hit [fol. 6r] **362** ok lemendr] *inserted above* **364** oc¹ ... **365** viðarretr] *inserted in margin*

They asked their wise men what seemed to them the wisest course and what they should do with the holy ark, whether they should send it back home or keep it longer.

Then the wise men replied to their questions thus: 'If you wish to send the holy ark back home, do not send it empty but honourably with gifts.

Now gather together from your five towns and make as an offering to God five gold rings and five gold mice, that the plague may cease, because it was a punishment to you all in common.

Make also a carriage fitting for the ark and a new box to contain your gifts, and take two young cows that have not come under a yoke, so that they may lead home the holy ark with the golden gifts that you are offering to God; and keep their calves tied up at home.

Then, if the cows are willing to go on away from their calves, you can know that it was the wrath of God that

afflicted you. If they are unwilling to go away

Hi axodon þa heora witan 465
hwæt him wislicost þuhte,
hu him to donne wære
embe þæt halige scrin,
hwæðer hi hit ham sendon
oððe hit hæfdon þær læng. 470
Ða andwyrdon þa witan
þam axiendum þus: 'Gif ge
þæt halige scrin ham
sændan willað, ne sende ge
hit na æmtig ac arwurðlice 475
mid lacum. Foð nu
togædere of eowrum fif
burgum and wyrcað Gode
to lace fif gyldene hringas
and fif gyldene mys, þæt se 480
grama geswice, for ðan ðe
eow eallon wæs an wite
gemæne.
Wyrcað eac ænne wæn
wurðlice to ðan scrine and 485
ane niwe cæpsan eowrum
lacum to fætelse, and nimað
twa iunge cy þe under iuce
ne comon, þæt hi þæt
halige scrin ham ferian 490
magon mid ðam gyldenum
lacum þe ge Gode geoffriað,
and healdað ða cealfas æt
ham getigede. Ðonne mage
ge tocnawan gif ða ky 495
willað gan forð on þone
weg fram heora cealfum,
þæt hit Godes yrre wæs þe
eow swa geswæncte. Gif hi
ðonne gan nellað mid ðæs 500

---

495 tocnawan] *sic* LRW, C tocwawan

375	Þa spurðu þeir at spaca menn huart fleirum þotte rað at fara með þui skrini heim eða hafa með ser lengr.	Then they asked their wise men whether most of them thought it a good idea to take the shrine to its home or to keep it longer with them.
380	Þa gerðu þeir þat rað aller at heim skildi senda; þa meltu þat hinir spakastu menn, 'Lotum fylgia með þui hinu helga skrini fagrar gersimar'.	Then they all advised that they should send it home; and the wisest men said, 'Make sure that the holy shrine is accompanied with fair treasures'.
385	Þeir toko þa til oc gerðu ringa or gulli oc [mys] or gulli.	They set to and made rings of gold and mice of gold.
390	Þat reðo þeir oc at gera skildi vagn oc beita firir kyr tver, þer er alldrigi kuemi aðr undir oc, sua vngar kyr þer er hinn fysta kalf hofðu boret, oc baðu taka þa kalfa oc setia inn, oc vita huert þer kyr vildi ganga.	They also advised that they should make a carriage and harness two cows that had never before come under a yoke, cows so young that they had born their first calf, and fix them to [the carriage], and see where they want to go.
395 400	Oc melti sua: 'Ef þer kyr uildi brott ganga fra kalfum sinum eða leið hina somo með þui hinu sama helga skrini sem heilagr domr var inni, þa vitum ver full	And they explained, 'If the cows wished to go away from their calves and [take] the same route with the same holy shrine that the relics were in, then we shall know quite

---

385 mys ... **387** Þat] messing or gulli, or gulli *deleted, emended from OE*

from here with the ark of God, then you can know that the plague was not because of God's wrath but occurred for some other reason.'

Behold, then the Philistines followed that advice and made five rings from their five towns and five golden mice, and built the carriage with all the contents and sent forth the ark.

Then the young cows yoked to the carriage went to the land of Israel, lowing loud after their calves, and nevertheless did not turn aside from the direct road, as if they

had understanding. And the Philistines followed the carriage to the land of Israel and left it there, and the pestilence ceased and the plague of mice.

Israel then also submitted with one accord to God, and God protected them against the heathen people and gave them victory so that they destroyed their enemies and lived in peace in the days of Samuel.

Here you can know about the heathen gods

Godes scrine heonen, þonne magon ge tocnawan þæt se cwealm næs forði þurh Godes yrre ac gelamp elles.' 505

Hwæt, þa Philistei þa fiengon to ðan ræde and geworhton fif hringas of heora fif burgum and fif gyldene mys, and macodon 510 þone wæn mid ealre þæra fare, and geforðodon þæt scrin.

Þa eodon þa geongan cy geiucode to ðan wæne to 515 Israhela lande, hlowende swiðe æfter heora cealfum, and ne gecyrdon swaðeah of ðan rihtan wege swilce hi gewittige wæron. And ða 520 Philistei folgodon ðam wæne to Israhela lande and forleton hit þær, and se mancwealm geswac þa and þæra musa gedrecednyss. 525
Israhel eac þa beah anmod-lice to Gode, and God hi ða geheold wið ða hæðenan leode and him sige forgeaf, þæt hi slogon heora fynd 530 and on sibbe wunodon on Samuheles dæge.

Her we magon tocnawan be ðan hæðenum godum

---

502 tocnawan] *sic* LRW, C tocwawan 521 ðam] [p. 312]
533 tocnawan] *sic* LRW, C tocwawan

giorlla at þat eitt olde vgagne þui er ver fengum.'

clearly that that one thing caused the disaster that we have experienced'.

Þa gengu þer kyr með þeim vagne til Israels landz, oc
405 beliaðu harðla at kalfum sinum, oc hurfu eigi aftr at heldr aðr en þer komo heim með þeim helga domæ sem hann hafðe aðr verit.

Then the cows with the carriage went on to the land of Israel, and they kept on lowing after their calves, and never turned back at all until they came with the shrine to its home where it had previously been.

410 Þeir hinir heiðnu menn fengu þa ar oc frið, oc batnaðe þa oc let af manndauða oc varane. En þeir I[s]raels þioð hurfu
415 einart til Guðs, en Drottenn var barg þeim val siðan, sua at þeir hofðu betr huar sem þeir komo saman með Samuels liði, er þeira
420 var byskup oc hofuðsmaðr. Af sliku megum ver vita huert megin þau hini

The heathen men then experienced abundance and peace, and things improved and the plagues and the warnings ceased. And the people of Israel turned continually to God, and our Lord protected them well afterwards, so that they flourished wherever they came together with Samuel's people, who was their bishop and leader. From this kind of thing we can know what power the

---

404 Israels] iraels *inserted above*
414 Israels] irraels

how little power they had over the almighty God.

They are not gods but are cruel devils, deceivers of souls and provokers of sins, who bring their worshippers into the broad fire of the torment of hell, from which they will never escape.

We all know well about the three boys from the kingdom of Chaldea whom king Nebuchadnezzar threw into the burning furnace because they would not turn to his gods from the almighty God who created all things.
God also saved them from the cruel king so that not even their hair was burnt in the fire, but they went singing in the roaring fire, praising their Lord and survived unharmed.

In that same land was the prophet Daniel, the chief servant of God, a man of holy life.

hwilce mihte hi hæfdon ongean þone ælmihtigan God.
Hi ne synd na godes ac synd gramlice deofle, sawla bepæcendras and synna ordfruman, þe heora bigængas gebringað into ðam bradan fyre hellicre cwylminge, þanon hi ne cumað næfre.
Us is eac fulcuð be ðan ðrim cnihtum of Chaldea rice þe se cyning *Nabugodonosor* awearp into byrnendum ofne for ðan ðe hi ne bugon to his godum fram þam ælmihtigan Gode þe ealle ðing gesceop.
God hi eac ahredde wið ðone gramlican cyning swa þæt furðon heora feox næs on ðam *fyre forswæled, ac eodon him singende on ðam* swegendan lige, hergende heora Drihten and ungederode þurhwunodon.
On ðam ylcan lande wæs ða se witega Daniel, Godes heahðegen, haliges lifes man.

535

540

545

550

555

560

565

---

549 Nabugodonosor] *supplied from* L **557** fyre ... **558** ðam] *omission supplied from* LR

heiðnu guð hofðu við varn Drotten er allz er valldande.

heathen gods had against our Lord who rules everything.

425 Þat varo eigi guð, þat varo grimmir dioflar oc salosui-carar oc upphaf allra synda, oc þeir fœra sina embettis-
430 menn i eld þann er alldrigi slocnar.

Those were not gods, they were grim devils and deceivers of souls and the source of all sins, and they led their followers into the fire that never dies.

Oc er þat fullkunnict huat sa hinn riki konungr er het Nabugodonosor [gerði]. Hann toc drengi þria þa er
435 truðu a einn guð oc gerðu eigi honum luta, oc let casta þeim i ofn brennanda.

And it is well known what the mighty king named Nebuchad-nezzar did.
He took three boys who believed in the one God and would not bow down to him, and had them thrown into a burning furnace.

En Guð getti þeira sua at þeir gengu þar i obrunnir,
440 sua at eigi suiðnade eitt har a hofðe þeim.

But God protected them so that they went in unburnt, so that not one hair on their heads was singed.

A þui lande hinu sama var sa propheti er het Daniel, Guðs vinr oc hans hinn
445 besti þegn oc heilagr maðr, sua at hann melti við varn Drottenn er hann villdi. En hann Daniel var með konungi þeim er het
450 Dari oc þotti honum allgoðr.

In that same land there was the prophet named Daniel, God's friend and his best servant, a man so holy that he spoke with our Lord when he wanted to.

And this Daniel was with the king named Darius, and everything seemed good to him.

---

433 gerði] *from H. edn*
444 vinr [fol. 6v]

Then in the days of Darius his councillors decided that for thirty days no man should ask a favour from any God but only from
the king, and thus they wished to ensnare the innocent Daniel, because he was very dear to Darius the king.

Then the prophet did as was his custom, went up to his garret and there fell to his knees and prayed to God on bended knees, until the heathens came, who had eagerly been keeping watch on him.
Then they betrayed Daniel to the king, saying that he despised the laws of all of them, and they wished to throw him into the lions' den.

Then the king agonised until evening, he wished to protect the prophet against them.
But when he could hold out no longer,
he had him seized and thrown to the lions that lay in the pit.

Then Darius the king said to the prophet Daniel,

Ða on Daries dagum *gedemdon his witan þæt binnan þrittigum dagum* ne bæde nan man nane bene æt Gode, butan æt ðam cyninge, and woldon swa besyrwian þone unscyldigan Danihel, for ðan ðe he wæs swiðe dyre Darie þan cyninge. 570

Ða dyde se witega swa swa his gewuna wæs, eode into his upflore and fel ðær om cneowum and gebæd hine to Gode gebegendum limum, oððæt ða hæðenan comon þe his cepton georne. 580

Hi wregdon þa Danihel to Darie þam cyninge, sædan þæt he forsawe heora ealra gesetnysse, and woldon hine besceofan into ðæra leona seaðe. 585

Ða swanc se cyning swiðe oð æfen, wolde ðone witegan bewerian wið hi. 590
Ac ða ða he ne mihte na leng,
ða let he hine niman and wurpan þam leonan þe lagon on ðan seaðe. 595
Ða cwæð Darius se cyning to Daniele þam witegan,

---

567 gedemdon... **568** dagum] *omission supplied from* LR
591 oð æfen] *sic* GL, C *of* hæfen, R *omits whole sentence*

455	Þa gerðu hans raðgiafar þat firir ofund er þeir hofðu við Daniel at konungr skilldi sua bioða at engi maðr skildi Guði luta nema ser goðs biðia til Guðs þria[tigu] daga; en þui vildu þeir Daniel suickia.	Then his counsellors, because of the envy they had against Daniel, caused the king to command that no man should bow to God, nor pray for a favour from God, for thirty days; and in this way they wished to betray Daniel.
460 465	En Daniel gerði sem hann var vanr, geck i loft sitt oc bað ser þar til almattegs Guðs; en þeir stiltu um huset er i ofund gengu við hann,	But Daniel did as he was accustomed, went into his upper room and prayed there to almighty God: and those who were against him for envy kept watch on the house,
470	oc sogðu konungi at Daniel gaf eigi gaum hans boðorðe, oc letu hann þess verðan, at honum veri kastat i grof þa er dyr in oorgu lago i siau.	and told the king that Daniel paid no heed to his commands, and they said that he was worthy to be thrown into the pit that seven fierce animals lay in.
	En konungren varðe þat mal oc quast þat eigi vilia, en þeir vurðu þo ricari er fleri voro saman.	And the king rejected the accusation and said that he did not want that, but they became more powerful as more gathered together.
475 480	Þa toko þeir Daniel oc kastaðu honum i grof firir dyr in vorgu. En konungr geck at sialfr oc byrgði aftr þa grof oc melti sua við Daniel: 'Nu hialpe þer þinn	Then they took Daniel and threw him into the pit with savage animals in it. And the king went there himself and locked the den and said to Daniel, 'Now may your God

---

458 þriatigu] iij, *emended from* OE

'Your God whom you worship will save you'.
Then he sealed the den from outside and was so sorrowful that he could not sleep all that night and he did not want to eat anything.

At daybreak the king Darius arose, went to the den and called out sadly, 'Daniel, you man of God, was your God really able to protect you against the lions?'

And he straightway answered, 'Beloved king, may you live for ever. My God forthwith sent his angel to me and he shut fast the lions' mouths with his bonds, so that none of them could harm my limbs, because in me is found righteousness before God, and because, O king, I committed no offence against you'.

The king immediately rejoiced greatly at this and commanded them to pull up Daniel quickly and then to throw in those who had formerly accused Daniel. And they were brought with their children and wives and straightway thrown into the pit,

'Þin God þe þu wurðost wile ðe ahreddan.' 600
And he ða geinseglode wiðutan þone seað and wearð swa sarig þæt he slæpan ne mihte on ealre 605
ðæræ nihte, ne he ætes ne gymde.
Darius þa se cyning on dægred aras, eode to þam seaðe and sarlice clypode, 610
'Danihel, þu Godes man, mihte la þin God wið ða leon ðe gehealdan?'

And he andwyrde sona, 'Þu leofa cyning, leofa ðu on 615
ecnysse. Min God me asænde to sona his engel and he ðære leone muð beleac mid his bendum, þæt heora nan ne mihte 620
minum limum derian, for ðan ðe on me is afunden ætforen Gode rihtwisnys and ic wið þe, cyning, ne worhte nænne gylt.' 625
Se cyning þa sona swiðe ðæs fægnode and het up ateon ardlice Danihel, and ða in awurpan þe hine wrægdon ær. And hi 630
wurdon þa gebrohte mid bearnum and wifum and into ðam seaðe sona

---

622 on me] C on ne *corrected to* on me **630** wrægdon] LR wregdon, C prægdon

Guð ef hann er sua goðr sem þu segir at hann se.' Oc gekk a brott i illum hug, oc matte huarke eta ne drecka ne sofa a þeiri natt.	help you, if he is as good as you say he is'. And he went away in a bad mood and could not eat or drink or sleep that night.

(line 485)

Þa gekk konungr þegar at morne at vita huat or Daniel veri orðet, oc kallaðe a hann oc melti sua: 'Lifir þu, Guðs maðr, eða matte þinn Guð þer hialpa við þessum dyrum hinum olmu?'
En Daniel suaraðe, 'Lifir þu konungr! Lifi ec harðla vel, firir þui at minn Guð sendi sinn engil til min en bant þessi dyr sua at þau matto eigi munni gina eða mer at angre verða,
firir þui at ec hafða ecki misgort við þic.'

Then the king went there the next morning to see what might have happened to Daniel, and he called to him and spoke thus: 'Are you alive, you man of God, or could your God help you against these savage animals?'
And Daniel answered, 'May you flourish, O king, I am alive and very well, because my God sent his angel to me and bound these animals so that they could not open their mouths or do me any harm, because I had done nothing against you.'

(lines 490, 495, 500)

En konungren fagnaðe þui harðla oc bauð sinum monnum at drega Daniel upp or grof þeiri, en hinum i at kasta er hann hofðu rœgðan, með konum oc bornum. En þeim var

And the king rejoiced greatly at this and commanded his men to pull up Daniel out of the pit, and to throw in those who had accused him, with their wives and
children. And they were

(line 505)

and the lions seized them and tore them limb from limb before they could even fall down.

Then the king straightway sent a letter throughout all his people and kindly greeted them in these written words:
'I wish that my people in all my kingdom unanimously bow down to Daniel's God and fear him. He is the living God, eternal in the world and his kingdom will never be overthrown in all eternity. He is the true redeemer and worker of miracles in heaven and on earth, who protected Daniel against the savage animals so that they could not harm him.'

Daniel continued then very dear to the king,
until king Cyrus came to the throne; and then Daniel became the king's table-companion and was honoured above all his officials.

There was then in Babylon the great city a god of the heathens who was called Bel,

aworpene, and þa leon hi gelæhton and heora lima totæron ær ðan ðe hi furðon moston feallan adune.
Ða sende se cyninge sona ænne pistol geond ealle his leode and hi luflice grette þissum wordum awritenne:
'Ic wille þæt min folc on eallum minum rice anmodlice buge to Danieles Gode and hine ondrædon. He is se lyfigenda God and ece on worulde and his rice ne bið toworpen on ecnysse. He is soð alysend and tacna wyrcend on heofonum and on eorðan, se þe heold Daniel wið ða ræðan deor, þæt hi him derian ne mihton.'
Daniel leofode ða swiðe leof ðan cyninge
oððæt Cyrus cyning to þam cynedome feng; and Daniel wearð þa ðæs cyninges gedrinca, and he hine arwurððode ofer ealle his þegnas.
Ða wæs on Babilone þæra mycclan byrig þære hæðenra god se wæs gehaten Bel,

635

640

645

650

655

660

665

---

637 furðon] [p. 313]
662 his ... **663** þegnas] C þegnas his *marked for reversal*

510 ollum kastat i hina somu grof, en dyrin toko við þeim þegar a lofte oc rifu i sundr þau oll.	all thrown into the same pit, but the animals caught them straightway in mid-air and tore them all to pieces.
Þa sendi sa konungr boð 515 þegar sinum landslyð ollum	Then the king straightway sent a message to all his countrymen
oc bað þeim segia sinn vilia at þeir skildu trua allir a ein Guð sannan, 'firir þui at ver vitum þat at hann er Guð 520 almattegr	and commanded them to announce his will that they should all believe in the one true God, 'because we know that he is God almighty
er slikar iartegnir gerði at hann helt Daniel við þui at eigi biti hann þau hin olmo dyr'.	who performed such miracles when he protected Daniel so that the savage animals did not bite him'.
525 Daniel var siðan lengi með þeim konungi oc þotti honum allgoðr. Þa varð sa konungr dauðr en annar feck konungdom þann en 530 sa het Cirus; þa varð Daniel en motunautur hans.	Daniel was afterwards a long time with the king and everything seemed good to him. Then the king died and another, who was called Cyrus, received the kingdom; then Daniel became his table-companion.
Þa var en i Babilon hinni miclu heiðit guð eitt oc het Bel; en þat sogðu þeir menn 535 aller er embettu Bel at hann þurfti mat sua mikinn at engi kunni þess dœmi. En	There was then in Babylon the great one heathen god called Bel; and all those men who served Bel said that he needed so much food that no one could estimate it. But

---

523 hin] hini **530** varð] var da, *H. edn* var **533** miclu] miclu en

and they fed him every day with forty sheep, and they gave him daily six measures of wine and twelve measures of meal for his sustenance.

The king honoured him and came every day to pray to the god Bel; and the wise Daniel scorned that Bel and always prayed to the almighty God.

Then one day the king asked Daniel, 'Why will you not pray to the god Bel?'

Then Daniel answered the king without hesitation, 'I will not honour man-made gods, but I believe in the living God who created heaven and earth and all things and has power over all flesh.'

Thereupon the king answered the prophet, 'Do you not really think, Daniel, that this wonderful Bel is a living god now that he lives by food and drinks every day what we bring him as offerings?'

Then Daniel said, 'Do not fall into error, king, this god is cast from brass on the outside and inside of clay and does not live by

and hine man dæghwamlice fedde mid feowertigum sceapum, and him man win sealde six sestras to þan dæge, and twelf sestras melwæs to his metsunge. Se cyning hine wurðode and com ælce dæg hine to gebiddenne to Bel ðan gode; and Daniel se snotera forseah ðone Bel and gebæd hine æfre to ðam ælmihtigan Gode. Ða axode se cyning on anum dæge Daniel, 'Hwi nelt ðu ðe gebiddan to Bele þam gode?' Ða andwyrde Daniel anrædlice þan cyninge, 'Ic nelle wurðian þa geworhtan godas ac ic geleue on ðone lyfigende God, se ðe heofonas and eorðan and ealle ðing gesceop and hæfð þone anweald ealles flæsces.' Ða andwyrde se cyning eft þam witegan, 'Ne ðincð ðe, la, Daniel, þæt ðes deorwurða Bel sy lyfigende god nu he leofað be mettum and dæghwamlice drincð þæt we him doð to lace?' Ða cwæð Daniel, 'Ne dwela ðu cyning, ðes god is æren wiðutan agoten and lamen wiðinnan and ne leofað be

540	konungr var til þess skyldr at fœra honum huern dag tolf sefsteri vins oc sald miols oc fioratigu sauða: þat skildi bera lata alt firir Bel.	the king was obliged to take to him every day twelve measures of wine, a measure of meal, and forty sheep: all that had to be carried to Bel.
545	Oc konungr geck þangat huern dag at biðia ser goðs til Bels; en Daniel sa enskis heiðar a Bel oc bað ser til eins Guðs.	And the king went there every day to ask for favours from Bel for himself; but Daniel despised Bel and prayed to the one God.
550	Þa spurði konungren Daniel, 'Hui vilt þu eigi biðia þer goðs til Bels?' En Daniel suaraðe, 'Ec bið mer aldrigi till þess guðs er þer hafet gort yðr, firir þui at ec bið mer til þess Guðs er lifir oc e man lifa. Huat man ec biðia mer til Bels dauðs?'	Then the king asked Daniel, 'Why will you not ask for favours from Bel?' And Daniel answered, 'I never pray to this god that you have made for yourselves, because I pray to that God who lives and will always live. Why should I pray to Bel who is dead?'
555		
560	Konungr suaraðe, 'Eigi þickir þer sua, Daniel, sem Bel se lifande guð meðan hann melir við oss oc matar nœytir?', quað konungr.	The king answered, 'Does it not seem to you, Daniel, that Bel is a living god when he speaks to us and consumes food?', said the king.

---

538 þess [fol. 7r]

food, and he never ate anything to this present day.'

Then the king immediately became angry in his mind and ordered the attendants who served Bel to come to speak with him, and he spoke thus to them: 'Unless you tell me the truth about this, about who consumes the food that we prepare for Bel, you shall all die, if I have any strength. If you demonstrate then that he eats the food, then Daniel shall suffer death, who criticised Bel and held him in scorn.'

Then Daniel spoke thus to the king: 'Let it be as you command, king.'

And they stepped into the temple. There were a hundred and seventy priests in all of those who served Bel in his worship together there.

Then they all said with one accord to the king, 'We will now all go out before you, king, and you yourself, if you do not believe us, may set the offerings before him and lock the door and seal the lock with your own ring.

And in the morning, when you go in and look, if the offerings have not been consumed by Bel, let our lives pay for it; and if Bel has eaten them, let Daniel then die, who so slandered him.'

metum, ne he næfre ne æt oð ðisne andwerdan dæg.' 705

Þa geswearc se cyning sona on mode and het ða bigencgas þe Bele þeowdon cuman to his spræce and 710 cwæð him ðus to: 'Buton ge me secgan þæt þæt soð is be ðisum, hwa ðas mettas þicge ðe we maciað Bele, ealle ge sceolon sweltan, gif 715 ic gesund beo. Gif ge ðonne æteowiað þæt he ytt ðas mettas, þonne sceal Daniel sweltan dead, se ðe tælde Bel and to bismore hæfde.' 720

Ða cwæð Daniel to ðam cyninge ðus: 'Stande ðin word, cyning.'

And hi stopon to þam temple. Ðær wæron hund- 725 seofontig þæra sacerda ealra þe ðeowdon Bele on his bigencge simle.

Þa cwædon hi ealle anmodlice to ðam cyninge, 'We 730 gað nu ealle ut ætforan ðe, cyning, and sete ðu sylf ða sanda him beforan and beluc þa duru, gif ðu us ne gelyfst, and geinsegla ða 735 locu mid ðinum agenum hrincge. And þone þu on ærnemorgen in gæst and sceawast, gif þas lac ne beoð bebrocene þurh Bel, beo hit 740 ure lifleast; and gif Bel hi geyt, swelte ðonne Daniel ðe swa hine hyrwde.'

565	'Nei,' quað Daniel, 'hann at alldrigi matarbita.'	'No', said Daniel, 'he never ate a mouthful of food'.
	Þa varð konungr reiðr harðla oc lastaðe sogu Daniels, oc bauð embettiss-	Then the king became very angry and denied Daniel's statement, and commanded all
570	monnum Bels ollum at koma til mals við sic, oc spurði at huat or þeim mat yrði ollum er borenn er firir Bel.	Bel's attendants to come and speak with him, and asked what happened to all the food that was taken to Bel.
575	'Ef þer segit mer þat satt at hann etr þat alt, þa skal drepa Daniel, er hafðe Bel at haðungu.'	'If you tell me the truth that he eats it all, then Daniel will be killed, who holds Bel in scorn.'
580	Þa melti Daniel, 'Stande þat þitt orð, konungr, oc rœynum vit huat satt er.' En þeir gengu þa aller til hofs þess er Bel var inni.	Then Daniel said, 'Let it be as you command, king, and we shall test what the truth is'. And they all go to the temple that Bel was in.

Then they all went out before the king and he himself placed the offerings before Bel; and Daniel ordered that they should sift ashes across the floor in the sight of the king, so that he could later know who had stepped on the floor to take the food. And the king quickly sealed the door.

Now the priests with their children and wives all went into the temple in the night by an underground passage and ate the food as was their custom, and drank all the wine, and their god Bel did not taste the offering.

Then in the morning afterwards the king went with Daniel to the temple and looked at the door: it stood sealed, just as they had left it in the evening.

They opened the door and looked in. Then the king cried out and said to the image, 'How glorious you are, Bel, and in you is no deceit.'

Hi eodon ða ealla ut ætforan ðan cyninge and he sylf gelogode þa lac ætforan Bel, and Daniel het syftan on ðæs cyninges gesihðe axan geond þa flor, þæt he eft mihte tocnawan hwa on þa flor stope þe onfenge ðæs metes. And se cyning þa geinseglode ardlice þa duru.

Hwæt, ða sacerdas ða mid cildum and wifum eodon into ðan temple under ðære eorðan ealle on ðære nihte, and æton þone mete swa swa heora gewuna wæs and þæt win eall druncon, and Bel heora god ne abat þære lace. Eft þa on ærnemergen eode se cyning mid Daniele to þam temple and ða duru sceawode: þa stod heo swa geinseglod swa swa hi hig on æfen forleton.

Hi geopenodon ða duru and in besawon. Þa clypode se cyning and cwæð to ðære anlicnysse, 'Mære eart þu, Bel, and mid ðe nis nan facn.'

745

750

755

760

765

770

---

747 Daniel] [p. 314]   **749** flor] C flor stowe: stowe *subpuncted for deletion* | he... **751** stope] *inserted above in* C   **757** under] *sic* GR, C urder   **762** Bel] *sic* GLR, C be   **767** geinseglod] *altered in* C *from* geingeglod

585 En þa toc konungr sialfr mat oc vin oc setti firir Bel oc rac vt þa embettismenn alla; þa toc Daniel osku oc saðe vm alt golf.	And the King himself took food and wine and set it before Bel and ushered out all the attendants; then Daniel took ashes and scattered them all over the floor.
590 En konungr lauc aftr sialfr durum,	And the king himself locked the door behind them,
oc geck vm morgonen at rœyna sogu Daniels.	and went in the morning to test Daniel's statement.
595 'Se þu nu, Daniel,' quað konungr, 'nu er matrenn allr ettinn er ec setta firir Bel.'	'Look now, Daniel,' said the king, 'all the food that I set before Bel is now eaten.'

Then Daniel laughed and stopped the king from going in and asked him thus:
'How does it seem to you now, king? Can you distinguish whose footprints you see trodden into the floor?'
Then the king looked and said to Daniel, 'I see in these ashes the footprints of older men and women and
children.' And he became angry then.

He commanded the false priests to be fetched, and they reluctantly showed him the door under the floor, where they came in and took the food that was intended for the god.
Then the king straightway commanded them all to be slain and assigned the god to Daniel's judgement. Then Daniel broke up the god and ignominiously destroyed the whole temple.
At that time there was living in that city a dragon and the Babylonians brought him food and honoured him as a god, although he was a serpent.

Then one day the king spoke thus to Daniel: 'You cannot say now that this is not a living god: pray to him, even though you would not to Bel.'

Þa hloh Daniel and gelette ðone cyning þæt he in ne eode and axode hine ðus: 'Hwæt þincð ðe, la, cyning? Hwæðer þu mage tocnawan hwæs fotlæsta þu geseo on ðissere flora astapene?
Þa beheold se cyning and cwæð to Daniele, 'Ic geseo on ðisum axum ealdra manna stapas, wifa and cildra.' And he wearð þa yrre.
He het ða gelæccan þa leasan sacerdas, and hi ða unþances æteowdon him ða duru under ðære flora, þær hi in eodon and þone mete ðigdon þe wæs gemynt ðan gode.
Þa het se cyning sona ofslean hi ealle and betæhte þone god to Daniels dome. Đa tobræc Daniel ðone god and towearp his templ unwurðlice eal.
Đa wæs on ðære byrig gewunod an draca, and þa Babyloniscan bæron him mete and hine for god wurðodon, þeah ðe he wurm wære.
Đa cwæð se cyning sume dæg to Daniele ðus: 'Ne miht þu nu cweðen þæt ðes ne si cucu god: gebide ðe to him, ðeah ðe ðu to Bele noldest.'

775

780

785

790

795

800

805

810

'Se her, konungr,' quað Daniel, 'spor manna er ec hygg at etit hafe mat Bels.'

'See now, king,' said Daniel, 'the tracks of the men who I think have eaten Bel's food.'

600 Þa geck konungr til oc sa þa beði þar vaxenna manna spor oc barna.

Then the king went there and saw the tracks of both grown men and children.

Þa nœyddi konungr þa til embettismenn Bels alla at
605 segia honum sanna sogu til huat yrði or mat Bels; en þeir mattu eigi þess lengr dylia oc sogðu hit sannasta at þeir hofðu sialfer etit. En
610 hann toc þa alla oc let drepa, en hann bað Daniel gera or Bel guði þeira slict sem hann vildi. Þa toc Daniel Bel oc braut allan i
615 sundr oc kastaðe i eld.
Þa var enn i borg þeira dreki einn sa er þeir hofðu firir guð.

Then the king compelled all Bel's attendants to tell him the true story of what happened to Bel's food; and they could no longer conceal it and told the truth, that they themselves had eaten it. And he took them all and had them killed, and he told Daniel to do whatever he wished to their god Bel.
Then Daniel took Bel and broke him all to pieces and threw them in a fire.
Moreover there was in their city a dragon that they held as a god.

Þa melti konungr við Daniel, 'Mant þu þess dylia
620 at þessi se lifande guð er ver blotum nu, þo at þu letir eigi Bel vera sua.'

Then the king said to Daniel, 'Can you deny that this is a living god that we worship now, even though you don't allow that Bel was one'.

---

622 letir] *repeated*

Then Daniel easily answered the king thus: 'I always pray to the almighty God, who is a living God; and if you will give me leave, I will kill this dragon without any sword or staff.'

Then Cyrus the king said that he might try out whether he could kill the dragon without any weapons.

Then Daniel prepared this offering for the dragon: he took pitch and fat and pounded them together, mixed with bristles, and he made it into lumps and boiled them well and gave them to the dragon.

Then as soon as he ate this food he burst, and Daniel said to the dragon's attendants, 'Now you can see who you worshipped.'

Then the Babylonians were deeply offended and came to the king in anger and said,

'This foreigner Daniel has taken your power and become king.

He killed the dragon and overthrew our Bel and killed his worshippers. Surrender him to us or we will kill you.'

Þa andwyrde Daniel ðus eaðelice þan cyninge: 'Ic gebidde me æfre to ðan ælmihtigan Gode, se ðe is lyfigende God; and gif þu me leafe sylst, ic ofslea ðysse dracan butan swurde and stafe.'

Ða cwæð Cyrus se cyning þæt he cunnian moste gif he butan wæpnum mihte þone wurm acwellan.

Daniel þa worhte ðan dracan ðas lac: he nam pic and rysl and punode togædere and mid byrstum gemengde, and berede to welerum and seað hi swiðe, and sealde þam dracan.

Ða toberst he sona swa he abat þæs metes, and Daniel cwæð to þam dracan bigencgum, 'Nu ge magon geseon hwæne ge swa wurðodon.'

Þa wurdon geæbyligde þa Babiloniscan þearle and comon to ðan cyninge and cwæðen mid graman: 'Ðes ælðeodiga Daniel hæfð ðinne andweald genumen, he is cyning geworden. He acwealde þone dracan and urne Bel he towearp and his bigencgas ofsloh. Betæce hine nu us elles we þe ofsleað.'

815

820

825

830

835

840

845

625 Þa suaraðe Daniel hogla konungi, 'Ef þu lœyfir mer, þa man ec drepa þann dreka er þer kallet guð, sua at ec hafa ecki vapn við.'	Then Daniel calmly answered the king, 'If you give me leave, then I will kill the dragon that you call a god, and I shall use no weapons for it'.
630 Þa lœyfði konungr honum sua at hann drepi þann orm oc hafðe ecki vapn við hann.	Then the king gave him leave to kill the dragon so long as he had no weapons against it.
Þa geck Daniel oc gerði honum mat. Hann toc bic 635 oc bustir oc istr,	Then Daniel went and prepared food for it. He took pitch and bristles and fat,
oc veldi alt saman oc gaf honum at eta.	and rolled it all together and gave it to him to eat.
Þa bolgnaðe hann allr oc brast i sundr, en Daniel 640 melti við hans embettis- menn, 'Nu megut þer sea a huern þer truðut.'	Then he swelled up completely and burst asunder, and Daniel said to the attendants, 'Now you can see what you put your faith in'.
Þeir vrðu [reiðir] borgar- menn aler oc letust ubota- 645 bol hafa fengit af Daniel, oc gengu aller til konungs, oc buðu honum koste tua: at hann seldi þeim i hendr Daniel, [elligar] skylldi þeir 650 drepa [hann sialfan oc] alla [hans] ætt.	All the citizens became angry and said that they had received from Daniel an injury for which no compensation could be paid, and they all went to the king and offered him two choices: that he should give Daniel into their hands, or they would kill himself and all his family.

---

627 er...kallet] ef þer kallet a
643 reiðir] reddir   **649** elligar ...

Then the king could not refuse them all but surrendered Daniel to those foolish people, and they threw him into the	Ða ne mihte se cyning wiðcweðen heom eallum ac betæhte þone witegan þam witleasum folce, and hi hine wurpon in to þam
wild animals. There were seven lions and he remained there six days.	wildeorum. Þær wæron syfan leon, and he þær six dagas wunode.
Every day previously they had given the lions two sheep for food and two dead bodies until then, but now nothing was given them so that they would tear Daniel apart.	Ælce dæg man sealde ærðan ðan leonum twa sceap to bigleofan and twegen leapas oð ðæt, ac him næs ða nan geseald, þæt hi tosliton Daniel.
There was then in the land of Judaea a faithful prophet named Habakkuk, who had ordered in reapers for his corn and was carrying food to them.	Ða wæs on Iudealande an geleafful witega Abacuc gehaten, se hæfde rifteras abedene to his corne and bær him heora mete.
Suddenly there came flying to him God's angel and commanded him to carry the food immediately to Babylon and give it to Daniel who was sitting in the pit.	Him com þa fleogende to færlice Godes engel and het beran ðone mete to Babilonian hraðe, and syllan Daniele þe sæt on þam pytte.
Then Habakkuk spoke thus to the angel: 'Now dear friend, I have never seen the city that you mentioned, and I do not know the pit and never heard it spoken of.'	Ða cwæð se Abacuc to ðan engle ðus: 'La, leof, ic ne geseah ða burh ðe ðu segst, ne ic nat þone seað, ne embe secgan ne gehyrde.'

858 dæg] [p. 315] **861** ða … **862** geseald] | nan … **862** geseald] *sic* R, CG *omit* nan **862** geseald]

En sakar [þessa] nauðar[kostz] toko þeir Daniel oc kastaðu honum i hina somo dyragrof er hann var aðr firir dyr in oorgu. Oc voro lion suelt aðr sex daga til.	And because of this hard choice they took Daniel and threw him into the same pit with the savage animals where he had been before. And the lions were starved before this for six extra days.
Huern dag skildu þau dyrlionen hafa tua laupa brauðs oc tiu sauði til fœslu; en tolf dœgr var þeim ecki gefit, til þess at þau skilldu Daniel eta oc honum grimlega bana.	Every day the lions were to have two baskets of bread and ten sheep for food, but for twelve days nothing was given to them, so that they would eat Daniel and kill him horribly.
Sa maðr uar einn i Iherusalem er Abbacuc het oc var propheta, en hann skildi fœra vercmonnum sinum fœslu, þeim er skoru akr hans.	There was a man in Jerusalem who was called Habakkuk and he was a prophet, but he had to take food to the workmen who were mowing his fields.
Þa kom engill Guðs til hans oc bauð honum at hann skildi fœra Daniele fœslu þa er hann hafðe þar til Babilon oc til lionagrafar þeirar er Daniel la i.	Then God's angel came to him and commanded him to take the food that he had there to Daniel, to Babylon and the lions' den that Daniel lay in.
Abbacuc suaraðe, 'Huert skal ec þa fara, herra min,' quað hann, 'er ec sa eigi þa borg eða hœyrða [ec] eigi sogur til.'	Habakkuk answered, 'Which way must I go then, my lord,' he said, 'since I never saw that city or even heard tell of it'.

(Line numbers: 655, 660, 665, 670, 675, 680)

---

653 toko] ‡ *unclear, explained above p. 116* **654** Daniel [fol. 7v] **672** Guðs] guðus **675** hafðe þar] þar *deleted; margin* ætlat verkmonnum sinum **676** Babilon] *inserted above* borgar **681** ec] oc

Then the angel caught up Habakkuk by the hair and swiftly bore him to the aforesaid city and to the lions' den in very swift flight.	Ða gelæhte se engel Abacuc be ðan feaxe and bær hine swyftlice to ðære foresædan byrig and to ðære leona seaðe swiðe swyftum flihte. 880
Then Habakkuk called to the other prophet, 'Daniel, you man of God, take this food that God has sent you.'	Þa clypode Abacuc to ðan oðrum witegan, 'Ðu Godes man Daniel, nim þisne mete þe to þe ðe God sende.' 885
And he straightway answered, 'Now my God, you were mindful of me and you do not abandon those who love you.' And he immediately ate what God had sent him.	And he sona andwyrde, 'Eala, þu min God, þu wære min gemyndig and þu ne forlætst þa þe lufiað ðe.' And he æt þa sona of ðære Godes sande. 890 895
After this the angel quickly carried Habakkuk the long distance back to his land.	And se ængel ardlice eft Abacuc ferode to his lande ongean ofer swiðe langne weg.
After that on the seventh day the king went sadly to the den and looked in;	Eft ða on þone seofoðan dæg eode se cyning sarig to ðan seaðe and beseah in to; 900
and there was Daniel sitting quite safe among the animals. Then the king called out and spoke thus to God: 'O Lord God in whom Daniel believes, how great and mighty you are!'	þa efne sæt Daniel ansund betwux ðan deorum. Ða clypode se cyning and cwæð ðus to Gode: 'Eala, ðu Drihten God ðe Daniel on belyfð, mycel eart ðu and mihtig.' 905

---

896 ardlice] *sic* GLR, C hardlice

685	Þa greip enggillin i har honum, oc flaug með honum, oc með fœslu vercmannana, til grafar þeirar er Daniel la i.	Then the angel gripped him by the hair and flew with him, and with the workmen's food, to the pit that Daniel lay in.
690	Þa kalaðe Abbacuc a Daniel, 'Tac þu uið feslu þessare er Guð sendi þer.'	Then Habakkuk called to Daniel, 'Receive this food that God sent you'.
695 700	En Daniel toc þa við feginn oc at, oc þackaðe Guði oc melti sua: 'Lof se þer, Guð almattegr, er engan firirletr þann er a þic truir, oc lœysir alla þina vini or nauðum, oc virðist at vitia min oc hialpa i sua mikilli nauð sem ec em nu staddr.' En engillenn toc þa Abbacuc propheta oc fœrdæ heim aftr til lands sins um mioc langan veg.	And Daniel received it gladly and ate it, and thanked God, saying, 'Praise be to you, O God almighty, who abandons no-one who believes in you, and who redeems all your friends from distress, and thinks to visit me and help me in the great distress that has befallen me'. And the angel took Habbakuk the prophet then and carried him the very long way back to his land.
705 710 715	Þa a hinum siaunda degi gecc konungr til grafar þeirar er Daniel var i castat i ryggum hug, oc vildi vita huat or honum veri gort, oc sa i grofena; en Daniel sat þa heill i grofenni milli dyranna. Þa meltti konungr oc quað þat hit fysta orð: 'Einn er Guð almattegr, sa er Daniel truir a, mikill ertu oc goðr, oc rikir oc ramr, er þu orkar þui er þu vilt.' En hann varð harðla fegin oc	Then on the seventh day the king went in a sad mood to the pit that Daniel had been thrown in, and wanted to know what had been done to him, and he looked into the pit; and Daniel sat safe in the pit among the animals. Then the king spoke and said as his first word: 'There is one almighty God, he whom Daniel believes in: you are great and good, powerful and mighty, and you accomplish what you wish.' And he rejoiced greatly and

And he straightway commanded his men to pull up Daniel from the animals' pit. Then he commanded them to throw in those who had formerly accused him, and they were devoured in a moment in front of the king by the savage animals. We could say much about such false gods,	And he het his menn sona up ateon Daniel of ðære deora seaðe. He het ða in awurpan þe hine ær forwregdon, and hi wurdon abitene on anre beorhthwile ætforan ðan cyninge fram þan frecum deorum. Fela we mihton secgan be swylcum leasum godum,
how contemptible they were and seduced their worshippers to all abominations and to endless deeds of violence,	hu bismerfulle hi wæron, and heora bigengas tihton to eallum fracodnyssum and to endeleasum morðdædum,
and he who did the foulest things was dearest to those gods.	and se wæs ðam godum dyrost ðe dyde mæste fulnesse.
Now our Saviour Christ came to this world in the sixth age	Hwæt, þa ure Hælend Crist com to ðissere worulde on ðære sixtan ylde,
and he taught the truth and illuminated the hearts of men with many wonders and revealed by miracles that he is true God when he arose from death through his divine	and he soðfastnesse tæhte, and mid manegum wundrum manna heortan onlihte and geswutelode mid tacnum þæt he soð God is, þonne he of deaðe aras þurh his drihtenlican

Line numbers: 910, 915, 920, 925, 930, 935

922 fracodnyssum] *sic* R, C fracnyssum **933** manna] *sic* RL, C mannum

	bauð monnum sinum at draga Daniel upp or þeiri	commanded his men to pull Daniel up out of the
720	liona grof. Oc let þeim casta i er Danielem hofðu rœgðan, en þeir vurðu aller þegar slitnir i sundr fyrr en konungr gengi fra þeim.	lions' den. And he had those who had accused Daniel thrown in, and they were all straightway torn to pieces before the king went away from them.
725	Margt kunnum ver oc aðrer froðer klerkar segia fra lausungarguðum; en nu er þat lanct oc leiðent at [segia] huessu illfus þau	Much could we and other wise clerks say about false gods; but now it would be too long and boring to say how malicious they were, and how
730	voro, oc huessu þau drogo fram sina embettismen til huersuetna er ilt var oc vmenska var i, til morðs oc til manndraps, til hordoms	they enticed their followers to whatsoever was evil and inhuman, to murder and killing, to adultery and every
735	oc til alskonar saurlifis. Þeir menn voro þeim guðum virkastir er mestar vdaðer e gerðu oc ferligast lifðu oc mest letu eftir	kind of filthiness. Dearest to the gods were those men who always did the most evil deeds and lived most monstrously and indulged in
740	likams fystum oc heimsens hœgoma. En var Drottenn Iesus Christus kom til þessa heims a hinni settu olld	the desires of the flesh and the follies of the world. But our Lord Jesus Christ came to this world in the sixth age, which is now current;
745	þeirri sem verðr, en fimm voro aðr gengnar: ein var Adams old, onnor Noa old, þriða var Abrahams old oc Moyses, fiorða	but five had previously passed: one was the age of Adam, the second was the age of Noah, the third was the age of Abraham and Moses, the fourth

---

718 bauð] baauð **728** leiðent [fol. 8r] **729** segia] *H. edn supplies*

power and ascended to heaven before a hundred and twenty people, men and women, who were witnesses to all the wonders that he wrought before them.	mihte, and to heofonum astah ætforan hundtwelf- tigum mannum, wera and wifa, þe his gewitan wæron on eallum þam wundrum þe he ætforan heom worhte.
You have often heard about the Saviour's wonders and about his holy teaching and	Ge habbað oft gehyred be ðæs Hælendes wundrum and be his halgan lare, and
how faithful he is to mankind, to those who scorn sin and love their Creator, because sinful worshippers are very hateful to him, because his nature is that	hu hold he is mancynne, þan ðe leahtras forseoð and lufiað heora Scyppend, for ðan ðe him synd swiðe laðe þa leahterfullan biggengas, for ðan ðe his gecynd is þæt
he loves purity. It would also take too long to say how his faithful apostles overthrew idolatry after the Saviour's ascension and banished by their power the depraved gods from the images where men had looked on them.	he clennesse lufige. Is eac nu langsum to secgenne hu his geleaffullen apostolas towurpan þone hæðengild æfter ðæs Hælendes upstige and þa fracodan godas afligdon mid mihte of heora anlicnyssum þær men on locodon.

Line numbers: 940, 945, 950, 955, 960

750 Dauiðar old, fimta
[herlei]ðing Gyðinga af
Babilonium; en vm þessar
allder matte engi maðr
koma til himirikis, er nu
755 ero taldar, til þess er hinn
helgi Cristr let hingat berast
af hinni helgu Mariu, oc
lœysti alt mannkyn fra
heluitis pinslum þa er hann
760 toc pinsl oc dauða a hinum
helga crosse.

the Age of David, the fifth the
exile of the Jews in
Babylon; and in these ages, as
enumerated here, no one could
come to heaven, until the holy
Christ let himself be born here
of the holy Mary, and saved all
mankind from the torments of
hell when he accepted suffering
and death on the holy cross.

---

750 fimta … **752** Babilonium]
inserted in margin **761** crosse
new chapter begins fra þui huar
huerr Noa sona bygði heiminn

SELECT GLOSSARY FOR THE OLD NORSE *DE FALSIS DIIS*

This glossary is planned on an assumption that readers of the text will have at least a fair knowledge of Old Icelandic based on regularised editions of saga texts, so it is largely confined to words and specific senses that may be less common in saga texts, and also to words that may not be immediately recognisable in the spellings used in Hauksbók.

Each entry has as the head-word the spelling that appears in the text so that, for example, *org* (representing *örg*, feminine of *argr*) is listed under *o*, not under *ö* or *a*, and *i* for regularised *j* is under *i*; this is followed in square brackets by the regularised spelling under which the word appears in dictionaries, the conventional grammatical abbreviation (with the gender for nouns), a translation appropriate to the context, and the line-number.

ar [ár] n. abundance H411
barg [bjarga] v. helped H416
batnaðe [batna] v. things improved H412
beita firir [beita] v. to harness H388
bic [bik] n. pitch H634
bra [bregða] v. deviated H76
braut [braut] f. road H214
bustir [burst] f. bristles H635
byrgði aftr [byrgja] v. shut up H478
cleke [klæki] n. disgrace H184
daðalaus [dáðalauss] a. lustful H175
dylja [dylja] v. conceal H608, deny H620
efni [efni] n. material H263
einart [einart] adv. continually H415
embettu [embætta] v. served H535
farsfullr [fársfullr] a. malignant H209
ferligast [ferliga] adv. most monstrously H738
firirfarast [fyrirfara] v. be destroyed H98
flerð [flærð] f. deceit H210
flerðarfull [flærðarfullr] a. deceitful H47
flimsku [flimska] f. mockery H102
frendkono [frændkona] f. kinswoman H183: 'he treated all his
    kinswomen shamefully and disgracefully' H182-84

fystum [fýst] f. desires H740
fœðist [fœða] v. is nourished H140
fœslu [fœzla] f. food H662, H670, H674, H685, H689
gina [gína] v. gape: munni gina, open their mouth H499
griote [grjót] n. stone H111
hannerðum [hanørð] f. skill H278
heiðar [heiðr] m. worth; sa enskis heiðar a: despised H547
heldr [heldr] adv., at heldr: at all H407
hernaðe [hernaðr] m. warfare H197
hogla [hógla] adv. calmly H624
hœgoma [hégómi] m. folly, deceit H741
iartegnir [jartegn] f. miracles H521
illfus [illfúss] a. malicious H729
istr [ístr] n. fat H635
kalla [karl] m. men H235
kostaðe [kosta] v. harmed H44
lastaðe [lasta] v. condemned, rejected H568
leiðent [leiða] v. boring H728
luta [lúta] v. bow; gerðu eigi honum luta: did not bow down to him H436
lutum [hlutr] m. part; morgum lutum: many times H68; sjau lutum: seven times H72-73
matarbita [matr + biti] n. mouthful of food H566
megim [megum] adv. (on both) sides H310
meineiðum [meineiðr] m. perjury H102
meinfullu [meinfullr] a. wicked H185
meini [mein] n. at meini: harmful H42
mikileti [mikil-læti] n. pride H114
motunautur [mötu-nautr] m. table companion H531 (for OE gedrinca)
mutu [múta] f. bribery H103
nauðarkostz [nauða-kostr] m. hard choice H653
nœyddi [neyða] v. compelled H603
nœytir [neyta] v. consumes H564
ofund [öfund] f. envy H48
olde [valda] v. caused H401
olmoso [ölmusa] f. good deeds H86
olmu [ólmr] a. fierce H493, H523
oorgu [úargr] a. ferocious H470, H656
org [argr] a. depraved H222, argar H236
orka [orka] v. be able to do H157
orostu [orrosta] f. battle H198
quensamr [kvennsamr] a. lecherous H175

rac ut [reka] v. ushered out H586
ramir [rammr] a. mighty H154, 715
ryggum [hryggr] a. sad H707
rœgðan [rœgja] v. accused H508
rœynum [reyna] v. put to the test, find out H581, H592
saðe [sá] v. scattered H588
sald [sáld] n. measure H540
saurlifis [saurlífi] n. filthiness H735
sefsteri (from OE sester m.) measure H540
selo [sæla] f. happiness H57
setia inn [setja] v. to pen up H393
skynsemdar augum [skynsemd f. + auga n.] n. with understanding (with the eyes of reason) H132
stein-spiold [steinspjald] n. stone tablets H317-18
stiltu [stilla] v. kept watch H463
suelt [svelta] v. starved H657
suiðnade [sviðna] v. was singed H440
tungl [tungl] n. moon; oll himin tungl: all the stars of the heavens H146
val [vel] adv. well H416
varan [varan] f. warning, admonition H358, H413
varliga [varliga] adv. warily H61
varna [varna] v. avoid H60
veldi [velta] v. rolled H636
vendi laust [venda] v. deployed (turned loose) H305-06
vgagne [úgagn] n. harm, affliction H402
vil [víl] n. misery H58
villudomr [villudómr] m. error H106, H153
viltir [villa] v. misled H243
virkastir [virkr] a. dearest to H737
vitia [vitja] v. (w. gen.) to visit H697
vorgu [úargr] a. ferocious H477, oorgu H470
vsattir [úsattr] a. obstreperous H123
ymisa [ýmissir] a. various H127
þverr [þverra] v. wanes H82
œrðust [œra] v. went mad (or [æra] v. honoured?) H226

BIBLIOGRAPHY

Following the example of McTurk, ed., *Companion*, and some other recent publications, the names of Icelandic authors are listed under the patronymic, not under the given name as in Iceland. In ordering entries, Þ follows T; prepositions and articles at the beginning of titles have been ignored.

Primary Sources

Adam of Bremen, *Gesta Hammaburgensis ecclesiae pontificum*, ed. Bernhard Schmeidler, 3rd edn, *MGH*, Script. rer. Ger. 2 (Hannover / Leipzig, 1917)

Ælfric's Catholic Homilies: Introduction, Commentary and Glossary, ed. Malcolm Godden, EETS ss 18 (Oxford, 2000)

Ælfric's Catholic Homilies: The First Series, ed. Peter Clemoes, EETS ss 17 (Oxford, 1997)

Ælfric's Catholic Homilies: The Second Series, ed. Malcolm Godden, EETS ss 5 (London, 1979)

Ælfric's Lives of Saints, ed. Walter W. Skeat, EETS os 76, 82, 94 and 114 (London, 1881-1900, repr. as 2 vols, London, 1966)

'Ælfric's version of *Alcuini interrogationes Sigeuulfi in Genesin*', ed. George Edwin MacLean, *Anglia* 7 (1884), 1-59

Alcuin, *Vita Willibrordi*, in *Passiones vitaeque sanctorum aevi Merovingici*, ed. Bruno Krusch and Wilhelm Levison, *MGH*, Script rer. Merov. 7 (Hannover, 1920), pp. 81-141

Alfræði íslenzk, ed. Kr. Kålund, Samfund til udgivelse af gammel nordisk litteratur [STUAGNL] 37 (Copenhagen, 1908)

Angelsächsische Homilien und Heiligenleben, ed. Bruno Assmann, Bibliothek der angelsächsischen Prosa 3 (Kassel, 1889; repr. Darmstadt, 1964)

The Anglo-Saxon Chronicle: A Collaborative Edition, 8, *MS F*, ed. Peter S. Baker (Cambridge, 2000)

The Anglo-Saxon Dialogues of Salomon and Saturn, ed. J. M. Kemble (London, 1847)

The Anglo-Saxon Minor Poems, ed. Elliott van Kirk Dobbie, Anglo-Saxon Poetic Records 6 (New York, 1942)

Audoenus of Rouen, *Vita Eligii*, in *Passiones vitaeque sanctorum aevi Merovingici*, ed. Bruno Krusch, *MGH*, Script. rer. Merov. 2 (Hannover, 1902), pp. 634-761

Barlaams ok Josaphats Saga, ed. R. Keyser and C. R. Unger (Christiania, 1851)

The Battle of Maldon, ed. D. G. Scragg (Manchester, 1981)

Bede, *Commentary on Genesis*, PL 91, col. 227
Die Briefe des heiligen Bonifatius und Lullius, ed. M. Tangl, *MGH*, Epistolae selectae (Berlin, 1910)
Burchard of Worms, 'Corrector', in Decretum Lib. XIX, PL 140, col. 974
Die Bussbücher und die Bussdisciplin der Kirche, ed. H. J. Schmitz (Mainz, 1883)
Byrhtferth's Enchiridion, ed. and trans. Peter S. Baker and Michael Lapidge, EETS ss 15 (Oxford, 1995)
Caesarii Arlatensis sermones, ed. G. Morin, Corpus Christianorum (Series Latina), 103 (Turnhout, 1953)
Clemens Saga: The Life of St Clement of Rome, ed. and trans. Helen Carron (London, 2005)
The Copenhagen Wulfstan Collection, ed. J. E. Cross and Jennifer Tunberg, Early English Manuscripts in Facsimile 25 (Copenhagen, 1993)
Early English Homilies, ed. Rubie Warner, EETS os 152 (London, 1917)
Elucidarius in Old Norse translation, ed. Evelyn Scherabon Firchow and Kaaren Grimstad (Reykjavík, 1989)
English Historical Documents: c. 500-1042, ed. Dorothy Whitelock (London, 1955)
Flateyjarbók, ed. G. Vigfússon and C. R. Unger (Christiania, 1860)
Gamal norsk Homiliebok, ed. Gustav Indrebø (Oslo, 1966)
Geoffrey of Monmouth, *The History of the Kings of Britain*, ed. Michael D. Reeve, trans. Neil Wright, Arthurian Studies 69 (Woodbridge, 2007)
Gísla Saga Súrssonar, ed. Agnete Loth (Copenhagen, 1956)
Hauksbók: The Arnamagnaean Manuscripts 371 4°, 544 4° and 675 4°, Manuscripta Islandica 5, ed. Jón Helgason (Copenhagen, 1960)
Hauksbók: Udgiven efter de Arnamagnæanske Håndskrifter No. 371, 544, og 675, 4°, samt forskellige papirhåndskrifter af det Kongelige Nordiske Oldskrift-selskab [ed. Eiríkur Jónsson and Finnur Jónsson] (Copenhagen, 1892-6)
Heilagra Manna Sögur, ed. C. R. Unger (Christiania, 1877)
A History of Norway and the Passion and Miracles of the Blessed Óláfr, ed. Carl Phelpstead and Devra Kunin (London, 2001)
Homilies of Ælfric: A Supplementary Collection, ed. John C. Pope, EETS os 259 and 260, 2 vols (London, 1967-68)
The Homilies of Wulfstan, ed. Dorothy Bethurum (Oxford, 1957)
Homiliubók, ed. Theodor Wisén (Lund, 1872)
Hrafnkels Saga Freysgoða, ed. Jón Helgason (Copenhagen, 1950)

Jocelin of Brakelond, *Chronicle of Bury St Edmunds*, trans., with introduction and notes, Diana Greenway and Jane Sayers (Oxford, 1989)
'Letter to Brother Edward', in F. Kluge, 'Fragment eines angelsächsischen Briefes', *Englische Studien* 8 (1885), 62-63
Martin von Bracaras Schrift 'De correctione rusticorum', ed. C. P. Caspari (Christiania, 1883)
Martini episcopi Bracarensis opera omnia, ed. C. W. Barlow (Yale, 1950)
Mírmanns saga, ed. Desmond Slay, Editiones Arnamagnæanæ, Series A, Vol. 17 (Copenhagen, 1997)
Miðaldaævintýri pýdd úr ensku, ed. Einar Gunnar Pétursson (Reykjavík, 1976)
Njáls saga, ed. Einar Ól. Sveinsson, ÍF 12 (Reykjavík, 1954)
Óláfs saga hins helga, ed. O. A. Johnsen (Christiania, 1922)
Old English Homilies, ed. Richard Morris, EETS os 29 and 34 (London, 1867-68)
The Old Norse Elucidarius, ed. Evelyn Scherabon Firchow (Columbia SC, 1992)
Otfrid, *Evangelienbuch*, ed. O. Erdmann, Altdeutsche Textbibliothek 49, 3rd edn (Tübingen, 1957)
Patrologia Graeca, ed. J.-P. Migne, 161 vols (Paris, 1857-66)
Patrologia Latina, ed. J.-P. Migne, 221 vols (Paris, 1844-65)
The Phoenix, ed. N. F. Blake (Manchester, 1964)
'Zum Phönix', in F. Kluge, 'Zu altenglischen Dichtungen', *Englische Studien* 8 (1885), 472-79 (pp. 474-79)
Pirminius, *Scarapsus*, in G. Jecker, *Die Heimat des heiligen Pirmin*, Beiträge zur Geschichte des alten Mönchtums und des Benediktinerordens, Heft 13 (Münster, 1927), pp. 34-73
Poenitentiale Pseudo-Ecgberti, ed. J. Raith, Bibliothek der angelsächsischen Prosa 13 (Hamburg, 1933)
Poenitentiale Theodori, in *Ancient Laws and Institutes of England*, ed. B. Thorpe (London, 1840), pp. 1-62
Postola Sögur, ed. C. R. Unger (Christiania, 1874)
Pseudo-Augustine, Sermo 'De auguriis', *PL* 39, cols 2268-71
Pseudo-Cyprianus de XII abusivis saeculi, ed. Siegmund Hellmann, Texte und Untersuchungen zur Geschichte der altchristlichen Literatur, Reihe III, Bd 4 (Leipzig, 1909)
Riddarasögur, ed. Eugen Kölbing (Strassburg, 1872)
Saxo Grammaticus: The History of the Danes, Books I-IX, ed. Hilda Ellis Davidson, trans. Peter Fisher, 2 vols (Cambridge, 1979-80)
Saxonis gesta Danorum, ed. J. Olrik and H. Ræder, 2 vols (Copenhagen, 1931)

The Scandinavian Runic Inscriptions of Britain, by Michael P. Barnes and R. I. Page, Institutionen för nordiska språk, Runrön 19 (Uppsala, 2006)

Scandinavian Runic Inscriptions in the British Isles: Their Historical Context, by Katherine Holman (Trondheim, 1996)

Snorri Sturluson, *Heimskringla,* ed. Bjarni Aðalbjarnarson, ÍF 26-28, 3 vols (Reykjavík, 1941-51)

Den Store Saga om Olav den Hellige, ed. O. A. Johnsen and Jón Helgason (Oslo, 1941)

Sulpicii Severi vita sancti Martini, ed. C. Halm, Corpus scriptorum ecclesiasticorum Latinorum, I (Salzburg, 1866)

Two Ælfric Texts: 'The Twelve Abuses' and 'The Vices and Virtues', ed. and trans. Mary Clayton (Cambridge, 2013)

Two Saxon Chronicles, ed. John Earle, rev. Charles Plummer, 2 vols (Oxford, 1892-99)

Vestfirðinga sögur, ed. Björn Þórolfsson and Guðni Jónsson, ÍF 6 (Reykjavík, 1943)

William of Malmesbury, *De gestis regum Anglorum,* ed. and trans. R. A. B. Mynors, R. M. Thomson and M. Winterbottom, 2 vols (Oxford, 1998-99)

Willibald, *Vita Bonifatii, MGH,* Script. rer. Ger. 57 (Hannover / Leipzig, 1905)

Wulfstan, *Sermo Lupi ad Anglos,* ed. Dorothy Whitelock (London, 1939)

Wulfstan's Canons of Edgar, ed. Roger Fowler, EETS os 266 (London, 1972)

Secondary works

Abram, Christopher, 'Anglo-Saxon homilies in their Scandinavian context', in Kleist, ed., *The Old English Homily,* pp. 425-44

—, *Myths of the Pagan North: The Gods of the Norsemen* (London, 2011)

Abrams, Lesley, 'The Anglo-Saxons and the Christianization of Scandinavia', *Anglo-Saxon England* 24 (1995), 213-49

—, 'Eleventh-century missions and the early stages of ecclesiastical organisation in Scandinavia', *Anglo-Norman Studies* 17 (1994), 21-40

—, 'The conversion of the Danelaw', in Graham-Campbell et al., eds, *Vikings and the Danelaw,* pp. 31-44

Bang, A. C., *Om Dale-Gudbrand,* Videnskabsselskabets Skrifter II, Hist.-Fil. Kl., no. 2 (Christiania, 1897)

Barrow, Julia and Andrew Wareham, eds, *Myth, Rulership, Church and Charters: Essays in Honour of Nicholas Brooks* (Aldershot, 2008)

Bekker-Nielsen, Hans, 'Frode mænd og tradition', in Bekker-Nielsen et al., eds, *Norrøn fortællekunst*, pp. 35-41

—, Thorkil Damsgaard Olsen and Ole Widding, eds, *Norrøn Fortællekunst: Kapitler af den norsk-islandske middelalderlitteraturs historie* (Copenhagen, 1965)

Beck, Heinrich, '*Hit óarga dýr* und die mittelalterliche Tiersignificatio', in John M. Weinstock, ed., *Saga og Språk: Studies in Language and Literature* (Austin, TX, 1972), pp. 97-111

Bischoff, Bernhard, *Latin Palaeography: Antiquity and the Middle Ages*, trans. Dáibhi Ó Cróinín and David Ganz (Cambridge, 1990)

Bjork, Robert E., 'Scandinavian relations', in Pulsiano and Treharne, eds, *Companion*, pp. 388-400

Blake, N. F., 'Rhythmic alliteration', *Modern Philology* 67 (1969-70), 118-24

Brown, Michelle P., 'Anglo-Saxon manuscript production', in Pulsiano and Treharne, eds, *Companion*, pp. 102-18

Bugge, Sophus, *Studien über die Entstehung der nordischen Götter- und Heldensagen* (Munich, 1889)

Blunt, C. E., B. H. I. H. Stewart and C. S. S. Lyon, *Coinage in Tenth Century England from Edward the Elder to Edgar's Reform* (Oxford, 1989)

Clemoes, Peter, 'The Chronology of Ælfric's Works', in Peter Clemoes, ed., *The Anglo-Saxons, Studies presented to Bruce Dickins* (London, 1959)

Conti, Aidan, 'The Old Norse afterlife of Ralph d'Escures's *Homilia de assumptione Mariae*', *Journal of English and Germanic Philology* 107 (2008), 215-38

Corrêa, Alicia, 'A mass for St Birinus in an Anglo-Saxon missal from the Scandinavian mission-field', in Barrow and Wareham, eds, *Myth, Rulership, Church and Charters*, pp. 167-88

Crawford, Barbara E., 'The St Clement dedications at Clementhorpe and Pontefract Castle: Anglo-Scandinavian or Norman?', in Barrow and Wareham, eds, *Myth, Rulership, Church and Charters*, pp. 189-210

Dronke, Ursula and Peter, 'The Prologue of the Prose *Edda* explorations of a Latin background', in Einar Gunnar Pétursson and Jónas Kristjánsson, eds, *Sjötiu Ritgerðir helgaðar Jakobi Benediktssyni*, 2 vols (Reykjavík, 1977), I, pp. 153-76

Dubois, Marguerite-Marie, *Ælfric: sermonnaire, docteur et grammairien* (Paris, 1943)
Eliade, Mircea, *Myths, Dreams and Mysteries*, trans. Philip Mairet (London, 1960)
Fellows-Jensen, Gillian, 'In the steps of the Vikings', in Graham-Campbell et al., eds, *Vikings and the Danelaw*, pp. 279-88
Förster, Max, 'Altenglische Predigtquellen: 2. Pseudo-Augustin und Ælfric', *Archiv für das Studium der neueren Sprachen und Literaturen* 116 (1906), 307-10
—, *Altenglisches Lesebuch* (Heidelberg, 1913)
Frank, Roberta, 'King Cnut in the verse of his skalds', in Rumble, ed., *Cnut*, pp. 106-24
Frankis, John, 'Languages and cultures in contact: vernacular lives of St Giles and annotations in an Anglo-Saxon manuscript', *Leeds Studies in English*, New Series 38 (2007), 101-33
—, 'Sidelights on post-conquest Canterbury: towards a context for an Old Norse runic charm', *Nottingham Medieval Studies* 44 (2000), 1-27
Franzen, Christine, *The Tremulous Hand of Worcester* (Oxford, 1991)
Fritzner, Johan, *Ordbog over det gamle norske Sprog* (Christiania, 1867)
Gatch, Milton McC., 'The achievement of Ælfric and his colleagues in European perspective', in Paul Szarmach and Bernard F. Huppé, eds, *The Old English Homily and its Backgrounds* (Albany, NY, 1978), pp. 43-73
Gerritsen, Johan, 'The Copenhagen Wulfstan Manuscript: a codicological study', *English Studies* 79 (1998), 501-11
Gneuss, Helmut, *Handlist of Anglo-Saxon Manuscripts: A List of Manuscripts and Manuscript Fragments Written or Owned in England up to 1100* (Tempe, AZ, 2001)
Graham, Tim, 'A runic entry in an Anglo-Saxon manuscript from Abingdon', *Nottingham Medieval Studies* 40 (1996), 16-24
Graham-Campbell, James, Richard Hall, Judith Jesch and David N. Parsons, eds, *Vikings and the Danelaw* (Oxford, 2001)
Green, D. H., *Language and History in the Early Germanic World* (Cambridge, 1998)
Gunnlaugsson, Guðvarður Már, 'Manuscripts and palaeography', in McTurk, *Companion*, pp. 246-48, 255-57
Hadley, Dawn, 'Cockle amongst the wheat: the Scandinavian settlement of England', in William O. Frazer and Andrea Tyrrell, eds, *Social Identity in Early Medieval Britain* (London, 2000), pp. 111-35

—, 'Viking and native: re-thinking identity in the Danelaw', *Early Medieval Europe* 11 (2002), 45-70

Hald, Kristian, *Personnavne i Danmark, Middelalderen* (Copenhagen, 1974)

Haugen, Einar, *The Scandinavian Languages* (London, 1976)

Helgason, Jón, 'Til Hauksbóks historie i det 17. århundrede', in *Opuscula* 1, Bibliotheca Arnamagnæana 20 (Copenhagen, 1960), pp. 1-48

Herlihy, David, ed., *Medieval Culture and Society* (New York, 1963)

Hill, Joyce, 'The dissemination of Aelfric's Lives of Saints', in Szarmach, ed., *Holy Men and Holy Women*, pp. 235-59

Hofmann, Dietrich, *Nordisch-englische Lehnbeziehungen der Wikingerzeit*, Bibliotheca Arnamagnæana 14 (Copenhagen, 1955)

Holtsmark, Anne, 'En gammel norsk homilie', *Arkiv for nordisk Filologi* 46 (1930), 259-72

—, *Studier i Snorres Mytologi* (Oslo, 1964)

Jakobsson, Sverrir, 'Hauksbók and the construction of an Icelandic world', *Saga Book* 31 (2007), 22-38

James, M. R., *The Marvels of the East* (Oxford, 1929)

Jente, R., *Die mythologischen Ausdrücke im altenglischen Wortschatz* (Heidelberg, 1921)

Jesch, Judith, 'Skaldic verse in Scandinavian England', in Graham-Campbell et al., eds, *Vikings and the Danelaw*, pp. 313-26

Jorgensen, Peter, *The Story of Jonatas in Iceland* (Reykjavík, 1997)

Kålund, Kr., *Katalog over den Arnamagnæanske Håndskriftsamling*, 2 vols (Copenhagen, 1892)

Karlsson, Stefán, 'Aldur Hauksbókar', *Fróðskaparrit* 13 (1964), 114-121

Ker, N. R., *Catalogue of Manuscripts containing Anglo-Saxon* (Oxford, 1957)

—, *Medieval Libraries of Great Britain: A List of Surviving Books* (London, 1964)

King, P., 'The Cathedral Priory of Odense in the Middle Ages', *Saga Book of the Viking Society* 16 (1962-65), 192-214

Kittredge, G. L., *Witchcraft in Old and New England* (Cambridge, MA, 1929)

Kleist, Aaron J., ed., *The Old English Homily: Precedent, Practice, and Appreciation* (Turnhout, 2007)

Kluge, F., *Angelsächsisches Lesebuch*, 4th edn (Halle, 1915)

Kolsrud, Oluf, *Noregs Kyrkjesoga* (Oslo, 1958)

Kulturhistorisk Leksikon for nordisk Middelalder, 22 vols (Copenhagen, 1956-78)

Larsen, Henning, 'Notes on the *Phoenix*', *JEGP* 41 (1942), 79-84

Leach, H. G., *Angevin Britain and Scandinavia*, Harvard Studies in Comparative Literature 6 (Cambridge, MA, 1921)

Levison, Wilhelm, *England and the Continent in the Eighth Century* (Oxford, 1946)

Lid, Nils, *Joleband og Vegetasjonsguddom*, Skrifter utgitt av det norske Videnskaps-Akademi i Oslo, II Hist.-Fil. Kl., 2 Bind (Oslo, 1928)

Lie, Hallvard, *Studier i Heimskringlas Stil*, Skrifter utgitt av det norske Videnskaps-Akademi i Oslo, II Hist.-Fil. Kl. 1936, no. 5 (Oslo, 1937)

McKinnell, John, 'The context of *Völundarkviða*', *Saga-Book* 23 (1990), 1-27

—, 'Eddic poetry in Anglo-Scandinavian northern England', in Graham-Campbell et al., eds, *Vikings and the Danelaw*, pp. 327-44

McTurk, Rory, ed., *A Companion to Old Norse-Icelandic Literature and Culture* (Oxford, 2005)

Mitchell, Bruce, *Old English Syntax*, 2 vols (Oxford, 1984)

Moltke, Erik, *Runes and their Origin: Denmark and Elsewhere*, trans. Peter G. Foote (London, 1981)

Müllenhof, Karl, 'Zur Deutschen Mythologie', in *Zeitschrift für deutsches Alterthum* 12 (1865), 401-09

Mustanoja, Tauno F., *A Middle English Syntax* (Helsinki, 1960)

Noreen, Adolf, *Altisländische Grammatik* (Halle, 1923)

Nordal, Sigurður, *Om Olav den Helliges Saga* (Copenhagen, 1914)

Page, R. I. and Jan Ragnar Hagland, 'Runica Manuscripta and runic dating: the expansion of the younger Futhark', in Audun Dybdahl and Jan Ragnar Hagland, eds, *Innskrifter og datering: Dating Inscriptions*, Senter for middelalderstudier, Skrifter 8 (Trondheim, 1997), pp. 55-71

Parsons, David N., 'How long did the Scandinavian language survive in England? Again', in Graham-Campbell et al., eds, *Vikings and the Danelaw*, pp. 299-312

Pelteret, David A. E., *Catalogue of English Post-conquest Vernacular Documents* (Woodbridge, 1990)

Pons-Sanz, Sara, 'Two compounds in the Old English and Old Norse versions of the *Prose Phoenix*', *Arkiv för Nordisk Filologi* 122 (2007)

Proud, Joanna, 'Old English prose saints' lives in the twelfth century: the evidence of the extant manuscripts', in Swan and Traherne, eds, *Rewriting Old English in the Twelfth Century*, pp. 117-31

Pulsiano, Phillip and Elaine Treharne, eds, *A Companion to Anglo-Saxon Literature* (Oxford, 2001)
— and Kirsten Wolf, eds, *Medieval Scandinavia: An Encyclopedia* (New York, 1993)
Reichborn-Kjennerud, I., 'Et Kapitel av Hauksbók', *Maal og Minne* (1934), 144-48
Roesdahl, Else, *The Vikings in England* (London, 1981)
Rumble, Alexander R., ed., *The Reign of Cnut: King of England, Denmark and Norway* (London, 1994)
Schomerus, Rudolf, *Die Religion der Nordgermanen im Spiegel der christlichen Darstellung* (Leipzig, 1936)
Seip, D. A., *Nye Studier i Norsk Språkhistorie* (Oslo, 1954)
Serjeantson, Mary S., *A History of Foreign Words in English* (London, 1935)
Seznec, Jean, *The Survival of the Pagan Gods*, trans. Barbara F. Sessions (New York, 1953)
Sisam, Kenneth, *Studies in the History of Old English Literature* (Oxford, 1953)
Storms, G,. *Anglo-Saxon Magic* (The Hague, 1948)
Swan, Mary, 'Preaching past the Conquest: Lambeth Palace 487 and Cotton Vespasian A. XXII', in Kleist, ed., *The Old English Homily*, pp. 403-23
— and Elaine M. Treharne, eds, *Rewriting Old English in the Twelfth Century* (Cambridge, 2000)
Szarmach, Paul E., ed., *Holy Men and Holy Women: Old English Prose Saints' Lives and their Contexts* (New York, 1996)
Talbot, C. H., *Anglo-Saxon Missionaries in Germany* (London, 1954)
Taranger, A., *Den angelsaksiske Kirkes Indflydelse paa den norske* (Christiania, 1890)
Taylor, Arnold, '*Hauksbók* and Ælfric's *De falsis diis*', *Leeds Studies in English*, New Series, 3 (1969), 101-09
Thomson, R.M., 'The library of Bury St Edmunds Abbey in the eleventh and twelfth centuries', *Speculum* 47 (1972), 617-45
Townend, Matthew, 'Viking Age England as a bilingual society', in Dawn M. Hadley and Julian D. Richards, eds, *Cultures in Contact: Scandinavian Settlement in England in the Ninth and Tenth Centuries* (Turnhout, 2000), pp. 89-105
—, 'Contextualizing the *Knútsdrápur*: skaldic praise-poetry at the court of Cnut', *Anglo-Saxon England* 30 (2001), 145-79
—, *Language and History in Viking Age England* (Turnhout, 2002)
Traherne, Joseph B. Jr, 'Caesarius of Arles and Old English Literature', *Anglo-Saxon England* 5 (1976), 105-19

Treharne, Elaine, 'English in the post-conquest period', in Pulsiano and Treharne, eds, *Companion to Anglo-Saxon Literature*, pp. 403-14

—, 'The life of English in the mid-twelfth century: Ralph d'Escures's Homily on the Virgin Mary', in Ruth Kennedy and Simon Meecham-Jones, eds, *Writers of the Reign of Henry II* (New York, 2006), pp. 169-86

—, *Living through Conquest* (Oxford, 2012)

Turville-Petre, E. O. G., *Myth and Religion of the North* (London, 1964)

—, *Origins of Icelandic Literature* (Oxford, 1953)

Turville-Petre, Joan, 'Sources of the vernacular homily in England, Norway and Iceland', *Arkiv för Nordisk Filologi* 75 (1960), 168-82

Tveitane, Mattias, *Den lærde Stil*, Årbok for Universitetet i Bergen, Humanistisk Serie 2 (1967)

Tyler, Elizabeth M., 'From Old English to Old French', in Jocelyn Wogan-Browne, ed., *Language and Culture in Medieval Britain: The French of England c.1100-c.1500* (York, 2009)

Þorkelsson, Jón, *Nökkur Blöð úr Hauksbók* (Reykjavík, 1865)

Unger, C. R., *Annaler for nordisk Oldkyndighed og Historie* (Copenhagen, 1846)

Widding, Ole, 'Skriften', in Bekker-Nielsen et al., eds, *Norrøn Fortællekunst*, pp. 27-34

Yerkes, David, 'The Old Norse and Old English prose accounts of the Phoenix', *Journal of English Linguistics* 17 (1984), 24-28

www.ingramcontent.com/pod-product-compliance
Lightning Source LLC
Chambersburg PA
CBHW030654230426
43665CB00011B/1089